Lords Hill

A Place Only God Could Save Me From:
Based On a True Story In a Small
New England Town

Colleen Bruce

Foreword by: Aphrodite Matsakis Ph.D.

Contents

Dr. Aphrodite Matsakis has authored over twelve books on an array of psychological topics, including post-traumatic stress, depression, women's issues, grieving, survivors of sexual and physical assault, suicide, family violence, vehicular accidents, combat trauma, and natural disasters.

Foreword

By; Aphrodite Matsakis Ph.D.

For centuries child abuse and other forms of family violence were shrouded in denial. Even in our own country, laws against animal cruelty existed before laws against child abuse. In the 1960's the silence began to be broken and today the problem of child abuse is widely recognized. However, to date, the emphasis has been primarily on child sexual abuse and, after that, on physical abuse. Yet the effects of other forms of abuse, such as emotional abuse and neglect, which are just as devastating to the human psyche, are often minimized, if not overlooked.

Hence the importance of this book, written by a woman who experienced almost every form of child abuse, from abandonment and physical abuse, to extreme forms of emotional abuse. Indeed, the verbal degradation she endured assumed almost gigantic proportions because it occurred in the context of a multigenerational chain of family violence and addiction, as well as in the context of a small town. Hence her family's problems became the object of vicious gossip and Ms. Bruce was subject to ridicule and bullying, not only at home, but at school, the village store and almost everywhere she went in her community.

In this compelling account, Ms. Bruce describes how she, a motherless child abandoned by her father, subsequently became subject to multiple forms of mistreatment, not only from her primary caretaker, but other relatives, some of whom were also abused as children or who suffered from an addiction or mental illness. She touches on areas of child abuse, such as emotional manipulation and exposure to adult sexuality and sexual depravity, which need to be recognized.

Ms. Bruce does not spare the reader some of the heartbreaking details of her experiences, yet there is not a shred of self-pity in her book. Instead she describes her abusers in their full human complexity, their good sides as well as their bad sides, often showing compassion and understanding as to why these people, like her unforgettable Nana and adulterous Aunt Charlotte, sought to cope with life by taking advantage of and disregarding the basic needs of an innocent child.

Yet, despite Ms. Bruce's insights into the origins of her perpetrators' abusiveness and self-destructiveness, she is more than honest about how these individual's damaged almost every aspect of her being, thus propelling her into years of addiction and other self-destructive behavior.

This book is humbly and clearly written. There are no long psychological complicated explanations, just the facts as she remembers them and her ref lections as an adult on a childhood that can only be described as pure torment.

It's amazing that she survived her past, not only in the sense that she didn't die physically, but in the sense that she overcame her addiction and the emotional blindness caused by years of trauma to the point where she could tell her story. Given the continuous nature of the traumas she endured and the fact she had to contend with not just one, but many, perpetrators, this is a monumental achievement. It's also noteworthy that she's grateful for what she did receive from some of her abusers, which has enabled her to survive.

Although there are scores of adult survivors of child abuse, there are few first person accounts of child abuse like this unique book. Many survivors remain in denial, addiction or other forms of escape, and are hence incapable of remembering their past, much less putting their past on paper in a coherent manner that can serve to enlighten others. But Ms. Miller has done so and her book, the result of decades of hard work and therapy and her own ongoing self-scrutiny, is a gift to us all.

*Some of Dr. Matsakis' books include; *"I Can't Get Over It, Survivor Guilt, In Harm's Way, Vietnam Wives, Trust after Trauma, Emotional Claustrophobia, Back from the Front and Rape Recovery Handbook. New Harbinger Publications, Inc. www.matsakis.com*

Dedication

First and foremost I want to thank my Heavenly Father for His Son, my Savior Jesus, and for His patience with me through many years of recovery.

Dr. Thomas Lynch, my psychologist, mentor, and friend, we lost unexpectedly in January 2011. His desire for me to write my memoir was at times even greater than mine. Thank you for all the faith you had in me and for the hope and healing you blessed my life with. The completion of this book is bittersweet for I know how illuminated your face and eager your eyes would have been to see its completion. God bless you, I loved you, my trusted friend and doctor.

Dr. Robert J. Mathes, there are no words or sentiments deep enough to express my gratitude, respect and love for you as a great physician and friend. Your testimony of the man and doctor that you are will resonate in the hearts of your patients and their families long after you're gone. I feel blessed and favored by God to have been one of them.

Dr. Aphrodite Matsakis, this memoir could have been written had it not been for your brilliant work with PTSD (Post - traumatic stress disorder). In 2004 when I found you, I was a walking landmine burdened with unpredictable triggers that would send me reeling out of control. You not only gave me an identity that I had searched for my whole life, but also the healing and recovery

I needed to have in my life. My affection for you will be deep and abiding the remainder of my days here on earth.

My husband, Michael, you are an angel sent straight from God. You have been my truest friend. The blessing that you are to me far outweighs any pain that has ever pierced my heart. I love you.

My girls, Marion and Elizabeth, I thank God for the gift of a precious and deep love unlike any I've ever known, the day(s) you were born. You've given my life more meaning and reason for healing than you may ever know. You have helped me to grow and learn humility. It is my prayer before I leave this life that you will know I've had the truest love in my heart for you.

June Y., Barbara M., Charlie C., Marion B., Earl T., Blanche V., Carl T., Katherine G., Donna Mc A., Doris A., D. Farina, and Pastor Lindsay you know who are. My life has been richer in love, friendship and growth because you cared, and shared so much of yourselves with me.

Introduction

For many years I've had a volcanic rumbling deep in my soul that would not be silenced. I knew that some way somehow, I needed to tell my story about the good and the bad that can come with living in a small New England town. Sadly, New England does not have a corner on the market when it comes to dysfunction. The multigenerational fallout that comes from child abuse, alcoholism, and adultery is universal and takes place the world over. It just so happens that my story took place in a little town I've called Lords Hill, located in the Lakes Region on the Maine and New Hampshire border. Our family settled in the area in the mid-1700s, long enough ago to just about get us under the wire to be considered natives. There is an old story that demonstrates a New Englander's mindset about being a native.

There once was a man by the name of Old Fred who used to sit in a rocking chair on the front porch of the general store. Dave, who had lived in town for about fifty years, approached Old Fred one day and asked, "I know I'm not a native, but all my children were born here. Doesn't that make them natives?" Old Fred paused a moment, pulled out the pipe wedged between his teeth, and said, "Well, let me tell ya, son. Just because your cat has kittens in the oven, it doesn't make 'em biscuits!"

Another not-so-popular reality in Lords Hill was, as my grandmother used to say, "In this town you wouldn't want to kick the paper boy in the seat of the pants—you might be kicking your own son!"

Unfortunately, over the past thirty years, Lords Hill has regressed; just about all that was once there is now gone. The big tannery that employed most of the village and folks from surrounding towns has been demolished. The only gas station is gone, and the lunch counter where breakfast, lunch, and ice cream were served went out a long time ago. All the community organizations are gone. Remaining buildings are in disrepair, broken window panes the evidence of a dilapidated society with nothing to offer its stagnant youth.

Growing up there, I learned a lot and lost a lot. Lords Hill was a little four-block town where speculation and talk were plentiful. My home life, more often than not, was like living in a house of unpredictable horrors, but it was also where I learned the value of a strong work ethic and how to be a good cook. It was where Ms. Polly taught me about Jesus during Sunday school and Vacation Bible School as she rocked me in her lap through my disruptive crying jags as a child.

The past twenty-two years of my life have been dedicated to healing from the traumas and addictions of my past and writing my life story has been a dream of mine for more years than I can remember. There's something powerful about knowing your life matters and you have a voice worth being heard. After I stopped wrestling with God over my deep-rooted codependency issues and let my guard down enough to let Him show me that both He and I could be trusted, I was finally able to feel real forgiveness and empathy toward those who had destroyed my childhood. Then the God I was so sure had deserted me then was able to fill the mother- and father-shaped holes in my heart completely with Himself.

I've tried to tell my story with as much balanced truth as possible. As someone who was very close to me was so fond of saying, "A guilty conscience needs no accuser." I am not here to accuse or judge any one. This is my perspective on my own journey. My truth, like everyone's, is as individual as every snowflake is in winter. I felt that the responsible thing to do was to change the names of my family members and the townspeople or omit them entirely. There with the grace of God I have gone and still continue to go. It is my prayer that in completing this book, I have honored the God of Heaven, Who has so many times saved me from the snares of self-destruction.

**Disclaimer: "If any part of this book resembles anyone living, it is by coincidence.

Colleen in 1968, one month before her mother's death.

CHAPTER 1

The Double-Edged Sword: Rescuing and Lashing Out

The sounds of whippoorwills, hoot owls, and crickets still remind me of summer nights in the small New England town where I grew up. My maternal grandmother bought an old farmhouse in Lords Hill shortly after my third birthday. It was located just around the corner from what we called "over town," the center of the village. Our house was directly across the street from the Lords Hill cemetery on the only main road leaving town. My three siblings and I went to live with Nana Hammond after the untimely death of our mother in a car accident, an accident that could have been avoided. Sometimes thoughts of my childhood there still haunt me, making me feel like hiding in a dark secret place where no one can find me.

Back in the 1960s through the early 80s, it was common for various halls in many of the surrounding towns to hold dances on the weekends. They were usually BYOB (bring your own booze), and people would dance, cheat on their spouses, find a boyfriend or a girlfriend, and occasionally fistfight. And I'm sure they had a lot of fun too. My mother had attended one of those dances on the night of her accident. She'd had far too much to drink when she left the dance hall. After side-swiping three cars and hitting a telephone pole head-on, my mother was gone.

At the time, my mother and father were divorced. My father had already moved on with his life and was getting ready to marry another woman who already had four children. He left the four of us behind like we'd never existed. When this second marriage didn't work out, he would marry three more times and raise a total of twelve children, none of whom belonged to him. Over the years my father would give these children, who did not belong to him, the best of himself and whatever money could buy, while never giving his biological children a second thought.

In fifth grade I remember calling my father, to ask if he could help Nana pay for a pair of eyeglasses I needed. At the time, he worked nights in a tannery: during the day he operated a roofing and siding business which he owned. Sixty dollars was all I needed. I can still remember how my heart sank when I heard his cold, abrupt answer: "No, I don't have it." He had somehow justified in his mind that our mother's Social Security death benefit included his court-ordered child support of forty-five dollars per week for his four children. He paid child support one month after my mother died and then he stopped. Nana wouldn't fight him for it, because she was afraid that he would try to take us away from her. She always swore up and down, "He'll beat you kids like he did your mother, and he'll probably molest you girls."

After I hung up the phone, my grandmother, hating my father the way she did, went on one of her rampages. She started swearing and ranting about him being no-good and how he had killed my mother just as much as if he had taken a gun and shot her. My father was apparently over my mother after the divorce, but she wasn't over him, and they'd had a fight before the dance the night she died. My grandmother blamed him.

To make matters worse, every time I saved up enough of my allowance or got some extra holiday or birthday money, I'd want to buy my dad something for Father's Day or Christmas. My grandmother would rant and swear every time she was driving me to his house to bring a gift to him. It always started off with, "He doesn't care if you kids are dead or alive, if you have a roof over your heads, or something to eat or not." Sadly he lived a mere twenty-five minutes away, but we were lucky if we saw him once a year. I just couldn't seem to accept that I had no parents to love me and the only one living didn't want me.

As a child, when we take our place on this earth, we have no way of knowing how experiences of trauma and loss will validate or invalidate the persons we become. My experiences mapped out patterns that I would follow for years. The way I was taught to believe and feel about myself and the world around me was completely different from the desire that I know today, God had planted in my heart.

I was nine years old when I found the newspaper clippings in Nana's desk drawer with pictures of my mother's car accident. Based on Nana's ranting, I had thought from the age of three until then that my father had actually shot my mother. To my recollection, no one had ever sat down with me and told me where my mother had gone. I can only remember standing in my crib in the corner of Nana's bedroom. It was dark and I was sobbing and gasping for air. I would be running my fingers back and forth repeatedly over the satin binding of my baby blanket. I can still see the bright light that would stream in through the partially open door of her bedroom. Nana and Uncle Henry, my mother's youngest brother, an alcoholic with schizophrenia, would be screaming at each other in the kitchen.

After my mother's death, my older brother, Jim, was the only person I remember holding and comforting me. He nicknamed me Ninny. He used to lie in my grandmother's bed next to my crib and reach through the bars and hold my hand, telling me that he loved me and that I'd be all right. Engulfed with intense anxiety, fueled by being in a constant state of fight or flight, I started to be affected emotionally, mentally, and physically as a toddler. Years

3

later in my recovery, I learned from my longtime psychologist, Dr. Lynch, that my childhood traumas had manifested themselves in various physical, social, and emotional difficulties. Phobias that had haunted me for years, physical ailments like migraine headaches, lower back conditions, fibromyalgia and nightmares as well as learning difficulties were all responses to the intense abuse that I had endured for an extended period of time.

A Pawn in a Game I Didn't Ask to Play

One of my mother's older sisters, Charlotte, lived over town in the middle of the village. She had a big hand in helping my grandmother raise and support us. We would have had some pretty sparse birthdays and Christmases, and very few school and winter clothes, had it not been for her. But it came at a price; she was an adulterous alcoholic who ruled everyone in her life with an iron fist from a self-appointed throne.

Being the youngest, I would often be taken along when she went out for the day. Knowing I would be excited, she would tell me we were going to spend the day together shopping and going to the beauty parlor, but usually she went to meet men and cheat on my uncle. Money, jewelry, cars, or use of their credit cards would often be the exchange. She'd have sex and a few cocktails while I sat, all dressed up in clothes she had picked out for our outing. I would wait on a couch or chair in some strange man's house, listening to them in another room, making noises which made me uncomfortable. Occasionally I would get a disturbing glimpse of my aunt's naked body down a hallway, passing between a bedroom and bathroom. I would be excited when she told me that the man's house we were going to would have a big pool and I could go swimming. Instead, I would sit and despondently stare out a sliding glass door at the patio and the glistening pool while she finished the business we had actually gone there for. I never made it to the other side of the door. My toes never touched the water. Heck, I never got to take my shoes off!

On the occasions when we did go to the beauty parlor, she would have them set my hair on rollers. When the hairdresser combed it out, my aunt would have her tease it and make it look like hers. As soon as I got home, after my sisters glared at me for getting what they thought was special treatment, I would go in the bathroom and stare into the mirror. I would be filled with rage at the image looking back at me. Grabbing a big hair brush I would start tearing at my hair until I had destroyed the puffy hairdo that made me look older than I was. By the time I was eleven I started using spray-in hair lightener—anything so I wouldn't look like her. Sometimes when she dropped me off, I would grab the kitchen scissors and run into the bathroom and cut off a bunch of my hair. I couldn't control what was being done to me, and I couldn't hurt the adults in my life like they were hurting me. Instead, I punished whom I could: myself.

When I started to be reluctant to go with her on one of her rendezvous, Aunt Charlotte would plan something special to keep me in her good graces. She would promise me that we would stop at the state park that I loved and have a special picnic. I liked it when we went on picnics, only because it was one of the few times she was real and wasn't getting drunk. She'd make what I called "clean-smelling" tuna fish sandwiches; they had no odor because she would rinse the tuna until there was no odor left. She made them on soft white bread and wrapped them in wax paper. We'd have cucumber sticks with salt and pepper on them and her homemade Tollhouse cookies were the best ever.

Sometimes she would tell me, "You are the daughter I never had, and I am the mamma you never had." Occasionally, when she was driving the car, if she was in a really good mood, she would reach across the seat and pick up my hand and say, "Let me nibble on your pinky finger. You've got pretty little hands, just like your mamma." I wanted so badly for her to be my real mother and all that to be true. I loved her, and she was beautiful to me from the first time I remember seeing her as a toddler. She had fancy dark brown hair and big brown eyes and thin lips that were always colored pretty with lipstick.

I was the happiest with her when we went on picnics and on the Saturday mornings when I would go to help her vacuum and dust. I was about six years old when I started to help her clean and put on holiday dinners and other parties. Sometimes when we took a break, she'd play records and teach me how to dance; if we were upstairs she would give me a quick squirt of her special perfume. I adored her.

However, by late morning or early afternoon after a few strong drinks of vodka or gin, being around her was like playing Russian roulette. I didn't know what was going to happen from one minute to the next. Sometimes, in the morning before she'd have her first drink, strange men would stop to visit. I would become transparent while she became sexually seductive, frequently by bending over the kitchen trash can with one of her short nightgown sets on, exposing parts of herself. If she was dressed, she would let them put their hands down the front of her blouse, or they'd huddle in a corner of the kitchen, kissing. Even as a child I would feel embarrassed for her.

Exposure Was Not an Option

One of the general stores in town was only two houses down the street from my aunt's. It was common knowledge—the talk of the town—that my aunt and uncle got drunk every night and had nasty fights. Their kitchen door would be open and they'd be screaming and swearing so loud that the people going in and out of the store could hear them. It was entertainment for whole the town. Some people used to sit on the store's front porch or just stand there and linger for a while to hear what was being said.

There was a lady in town that would corner me like a rat every time I went to play with her daughter. I was about nine years old when she starting asking me, "What do you think your aunt is doing with all those men?" I'd freeze. When she figured I was old enough to know what was going on with my aunt and her "male friends," her questions and comments became more direct, cruel, and judgmental. Knowing I couldn't deny it, I felt like she derived some kind of perverse pleasure out of having the opportunity to tear my family down to my face. This woman was known for years by everyone as the town gossip. What she didn't know she'd improvise. Regardless of whom she embarrassed or whose life and reputation she destroyed. She'd make up blatant lies – just to fill in the blanks...

One day when I was about ten years old, my cousins, a couple of friends, and I were in front of the store riding our bicycles on the sidewalk. There was a big German man who lived on the steep hill across the river. He was a mean drunk and had come to town to buy what was called back then a pack of beer. His face beet red, he came strutting out of the store half drunk. Throwing out his chest, he walked over to me; and with his big mauling hand, he shoved a dime into mine and said in a roaring voice, "Here, little girl. Give me a call if you're going to be a tramp like your aunt when you grow up." Sadly, words and actions like these, from various people in my life, not only upset me as a child, but also gave give me guilty, dirty feelings for years to come.

But fate, karma, or whatever one chooses to call it—personally, I prefer reaping and sowing— it usually wins. As a much younger man, that big German had gone off to war. He had five girls but always wanted a son. As the story goes, while he was away, the wife he verbally and physically abused got pregnant and had a son—perhaps by a man who treated her a little more gently.. When he returned he made her put the baby out on the porch to sleep until he could be given up for adoption. But adoption day never came, and the little boy died of pneumonia. Shortly after that he got his own son, but the poor boy was born mentally and physically challenged. Being the outraged alcoholic he was, he proceeded to abuse his wife and boy even worse.

As it would turn out, this boy, who wasn't expected to live to be very old, far outlived his father. He was loved, adored, and looked after by the generations of townspeople for fifty miles around. The men's local softball league always gave him a place on the team. They'd take him on the bus to out-of-town games and treat him to a few beers at the local pub. Two of the German's brothers received medals after the war, but I don't remember hearing anything about him ever being honored for his to service to his country. The majority of the townspeople avoided the old drunken German like the plague, because he was always looking for a fight. Most of his own family either feared him or hated him and would eventually have nothing to do with him at all.

Don't Throw the Babies Out with the Bath Water

There was no amount of gifts, shopping sprees, or hairdos my Aunt Charlotte could give me that would undo the adulterous thoughts and actions she had exposed me to. When I was eight years old, I started resisting her passive aggressiveness. Arrogantly she would threaten me by saying, "I will go get the little girls up the street to love me, go places, and do nice things with me." This went on for several years. Then one day I realized there was no little girl up the street or anywhere else for that matter. But plan B was around the corner.

Aunt Charlotte was in the early stages of lupus, which was affecting her lungs. Unfortunately it didn't slow down her drinking at all. Typically she would drink until she vomited and needed oxygen for an hour or so. Every time this happened it would instantly throw me into a state of panic and she knew it. Plan B would start to ensue. Frantically, I'd help clean up the majority of the mess after the big Sunday or holiday dinner, or party she had just had. Then I'd race upstairs to find her lying on her bed with an oxygen mask on. She would stare at me intensely from behind the mask with glossy and pitiful eyes. Meanwhile, her chest and body would be heaving up and down like she was going to die.

I'd stand at the foot of her bed, filled with fear that she would die and leave me like my mother had. On the verge of bawling my eyes out, I'd hear her say, "Oh, Sissy, don't leave me. I love you. I don't know what I'd do without you. You are all I have." I believed her. And through the years, even when I felt resentment and anger towards her, I believed it. I believed it until the day she died.

Years ago, I wished hate and resentment could erase the pain and losses I had suffered, caused by someone else's actions, words, and deeds. But, it doesn't work that way. Instead over the years I have strived to remember those who have hurt me, have their stories, too. All I know is I loved my aunt and grandmother, despite the hurtful things they did and said. I really did.

Over twenty years later, shortly before my aunt died, we went out for lunch one day to her favorite restaurant on the Seacoast. Our roles had seemed to reverse. She no longer drank; I had done my share. I was a mother of two and had been in counseling for quite some time. It was evident that I had grown up. The playing field seemed more even now. Sadly she had become frail; her lupus was catching up with her. But she was still beautiful to me.

She continued to fix her hair every day, wear lipstick and jewelry, and dress stylishly.

While we were waiting for dessert, she looked across the table at me in a way I'd never seen before and said, "Sissy, I just want you to know, you are a much better mamma to your children than I ever was to you." As I fought back the tears welling up in my eyes and a lump that wouldn't budge from my throat, I tried to stop her. Affectionately, I tried telling her that it was okay. She didn't need to say that.

"No," she said. "You're a much better person and wife than I've ever been. I just want you to know how proud I am of the woman you've become." In that moment, I received the greatest gift that she had ever given me. Money couldn't buy it, and her death couldn't take it away. As tears streamed down my face, I was torn by feelings of resentment towards God and her, because this moment had come so late in my life and hers. At the same time, I felt pure joy and a sense of relief. I had witness what I had waited years for, a goodness in her that was real and abiding.

Over the years she belonged to various organizations. When some of the people from these groups would see me, they'd always tell me, "Your Aunt Charlotte is so proud of you and what you've done with your life! She raves about what a good cook and mother you are and how you're always working so hard. She just can't say enough good things about you." All the while, it seemed they were anticipating some kind of a nasty tongue-lashing about her from me. Regretfully, this sometimes happened, especially in my younger years before I started counseling. Then one day I realized very few people were sharing sincerely. They knew the score between her and me. It's always disappointed me, how some people get pleasure out of shortening your pencil, to make theirs look longer.

Aunt Charlotte died a few months after our luncheon. She passed away in her living room chair. I drove to the hospital where she had been taken in the middle of the night. I just had to see her. As I walked down the long, cold and empty hall to the morgue, the nurse escorting me started questioning me. "Are you sure you can handle this?" My childhood had left very little fear in me. I assured her I would be fine. Slowly the nurse pulled out the steel table that they had laid her on. Calmly I looked upon her face as she lay there in her favorite soft yellow sweater with a delicately scalloped edge. She was wearing the matching earrings and necklace that I had bought her. I couldn't seem to make one tear fall. Desperation was all I could feel. I felt like I was looking at a distant stranger. This was a woman I had loved my whole life, with my all heart. Yet, I had never really known her.

That fall as the crisp air of autumn blew through my soul, once again I found myself struggling with another season of pain and loss. Except this time I would be void of any real grieving for Aunt Charlotte for years to come. I believe my relationship with her had been like an abusive marriage or any other dysfunctional relationship for that matter. Over the years she had killed everything inside of me to the point where her death was as much a relief as it was a sorrow.

CHAPTER 2

The Roots of Unhappiness

Trying to cope with to the emotional pain that my grandmother often inf licted on me was something I just could never get used to. Strangely enough, I always knew she loved us. It would be years after she was gone, when I had two children of my own and was married to an emotionally abusive and passive-aggressive alcoholic, that I could have a greater appreciation for the challenges she often faced. Especially as a child and teenager, it was easy for me to judge and resent her. But there's something about age and experience, or at least there should be, that helps us to see people and events in a more merciful light.

By the time my second daughter was born, I realized that for a widowed woman of sixty-four raising four young children ranging in age from three to eleven was quite an undertaking. Nana was already caring for her elderly mother. A woman that had not wanted her and made no bones about it while she was growing up. My grandmother was an only child. When people would ask her mother if she was the only one, my great-grandmother would always answer, "Yes, and enough of the kind."

My mother was the fourth of Nana's ten children that she would bury before her own death in 1982. Two of the other three children that died were girls she lost in infancy. One of them died of crib death, better known today as SIDS. The other little girl died from as what Nana called, "a blue baby." She turned blue and died in my grandmother's arms while she was breastfeeding her. The third child was a little boy five years old, tragically killed by a piece of farm machinery that rolled down a hill, as Nana watched helplessly from the kitchen window. Sadly, when she lost each one of these children, her mother would say, "This happened because God is punishing you for being such a tramp. And you probably don't know who the real father is."

The Child Who Wouldn't Punish His Mother

My great-grandmother chose Nana's first husband, with whom she had her first baby, a little boy they named Frank. The marriage lasted less than two years. Curiously her mother took it upon herself to decide that my grandmother didn't deserve to keep the little boy. Abruptly my great-grandmother took Frank away from Nana, and he never lived with her again. She was allowed to have him occasionally for day visits on the weekends, or to take him shopping for clothes and shoes. When my Uncle Frank was older, he told in his own words how my great-grandfather, had made a living off his back for years.

In a resentful tone, he'd say, "My grandfather would take all kinds of jobs; everything from working in the woods and haying fields to butchering animals. He'd help some with the butchering. But, as far as the other work was concerned, he did as little as possible." Uncle Frank and his simple-minded cousin who boarded with them were expected to do the bulk of the work. My great-grandfather would collect the pay, and Uncle Frank and his cousin were lucky if they realized a penny of it. The irony of this whole saga would be that despite the reality that my great-grandmother never wanted Nana, the older my uncle Frank got, the more a dead ringer for his mother he became, right down to his hands.

When Frank became an adult, he was the only one of all Nana's living children who didn't argue with her or make her feel guilty. To the best of my knowledge, he never held any animosity against her or one ounce of jealousy toward his siblings. He did everything he could to help her and expected nothing in return. He kept her cars fixed so she could stay on the road with us kids.

Uncle Frank and his wife, Aunt Dorothy, lived not too far over the Maine border. It seemed they were the only relatives we had that never minded Nana bringing all of us to visit to have meals with them. Cheerfully they welcomed us as many weekends

a month as we wanted or anytime in between. I was happier there than anywhere else in the world. Uncle Frank's property was filled with lots of old iron and outbuildings that were so full of stuff and junk that there was barely a path to get inside them. Scattered about the fields were old, broken-down cars, trucks, and tractors that still had steering wheels and shifters. I would spend hours at a time playing in one, pretending to drive.

Meanwhile, Aunt Dorothy would be in the house making biscuits and chocolate cake and frying up fresh breaded zucchinis from the garden. Uncle Frank butchered pigs every fall, so pork was usually part of our Sunday dinner. If we stayed late enough we'd catch a glimpse of Aunt Dorothy's hair set in rollers, so all she'd have to do is comb it out for work the next morning. She used pink hairdressing tape to hold down her bags and the hair on the nape of neck. She was a small woman and as cute as a button.

Aunt Dorothy was a wonderful cake decorator. For many years my sisters and I were recipients of beautiful birthday cakes thanks to her. The only thing that every really "got her goat" as we say here in New England, was when we would steal her roses and daisies that were made out of frosting. She kept quite a charge of them made ahead for cake orders. They were stored in plastic containers on a rack in the shed off the kitchen. It was hard to pass through there and not pop the corner up on one of those containers and snitch a rose or daisy.

Occasionally Uncle Frank would pay me five cents a grain bag to collect pinecones around the yard; he used them to start fires in the fireplace on the back porch. Other times I'd spend hours out in the garage watching him and his oldest son work on Nana's car. That was when he'd offer me a puff off his corncob pipe. He used to say, "Here, you wanna smock?" During our visits, we would make a dozen trips through the mud room that connected the garage to Aunt Dorothy's kitchen. Uncle Frank cleaned department stores for a living, and he'd bring home all kinds unwrapped candy that were going to be thrown out. Neatly it was stored in big metal trash cans in the mud room. We'd eat our fill while we were there. Then when it was time to go home, no one ever made any mention of our bulging pants pockets.

Their home gave us the temporary illusion of freedom from the trials and heartaches that we were facing at home. It was the only place where I could be both real and a child. My aunt and uncle were hard workers, but they didn't push us, and there was very little upheaval in their home. It always felt like the other people in my life gave or withheld their love in order to control me. But they loved us, and they meant it. They are both gone now, but my heart will forever be filled with love and admiration for them.

Shortly after Nana's divorce from her first husband, she married my grandfather, who was twenty-eight years her senior. She was twenty-one at the time. When her mother found out about the marriage, she horsewhipped my grandmother at the local county fair. It would be putting it mildly to say that the road was always a hard one for Nana when it came to her mother.

My great-grandmother would often babysit me while Nana worked. One day when I was about six, she fell asleep on the couch. I wanted a drink but couldn't reach the cupboard where Nana kept the tumblers. Quietly, I climbed up on the old soapstone sink in the kitchen and grabbed the edge of the metal medicine cabinet that hung over it. In short order I ended up slicing my finger badly on the sharp edge.

Frightened, I went running to wake my great-grandmother up. I started shaking her, but I couldn't make her come to. I ran screeching down the front hall, hollering to Uncle Henry who was upstairs in his room. We had no phone at the time. My mother had run a phone bill up so high before she died that four years later, Nana still hadn't paid it off. Unfortunately, Nana was the only person in the house who drove a car. Uncle Henry stood over my great-grandmother anxiously yelling her name trying to wake her up, but, to no avail. Frantically, Uncle Henry hitched up his old paint horse, Chico, to the wagon and went over town to get Aunt Charlotte. The ambulance came and took her away. She had had a bad stroke. I never saw her again.

Surprisingly, my great-grandmother was always good to me. She bought the first bike I ever had. It was a fancy red tricycle with a loud horn on one of the handlebars. I used to ride it every time we walked over town.It sported a basket on the front that was big enough to hold the mail, her purchases from the store, and so much candy that I didn't have a good tooth left in my head by the time she died. But the relationships between her and Uncle Henry and my two older sisters were terrible. Uncle Henry abused my great-grandmother verbally, often raising his hand to strike her. In turn, she abused my sisters, frequently by pulling them around the living room by the hair or trying to get them in trouble with Nana for something she had done.

She Did the Best She Could

My Grandmother, Hammond, was an equal-opportunity punisher, except when it came to my oldest sibling, Jim. She always

Colleen Bruce

favored boys over girls, and he could do no wrong. Subsequently, we girls got our fair share of the razor strap and often his share, too. If it involved Jim, it was always our fault. Nana's razor strap was two thick pieces of long leather held together by a big metal ring. It hung on a hook behind the cellar door. When she went for that strap, we knew she meant business.

She never hit us in the face. But every time that strap hit you, she'd be calling me every filthy name in the book. Quite often, I would end up with welts on my legs that would last a week. Nana could do and say whatever she wanted to us. If anyone else hurt us, unless it was Uncle Henry, she could take the roof off a building! That razor strap never hurt as bad as the degrading things that spewed out of her mouth.

In other ways, she cared. Nana taught us about things that many of our friend's parents didn't seem to pay much attention to. At our house food was plentiful and always available. My grandmother could make a meal fit for a king out of little or nothing. She didn't care what we took to eat, as long as we didn't waste it. With our family, food was used for everything from celebration to compensation. I started having a compulsive eating disorder by the time I was five. Rarely, did I have the right to express my feelings. When I did, I got punished, so I ate. I would eat until my stomach was hard as a rock. Usually, it hurt so badly I could hardly move. The only thing that gave me any relief was to lie flat on my stomach on a thin rug that covered the wooden floor in the living room. Beneath it was a dirt cellar. Cool, damp air would seep through the cracks in the floor, making my stomach feel better.

At supper time it didn't matter what Nana made, we kids always ate first. If there wasn't enough left for her, she'd have a cup of tea and a biscuit with molasses or peanut butter on it. Some of our relatives would ask her to come over to their house for a meal or cookout; either they didn't want all of us kids or they wanted to feed us something different from what the adults were having. I remember a time when one of my uncles got really mad at her; he had bought lobster and steak for the adults and hotdogs for their children and us kids. When my grandmother wouldn't eat anything but a hotdog, he was furious. She said, "No. You let me tell you something, I eat what my kids eat. If they eat hotdogs, I eat hotdogs!"

Nana cooked all the time—for Grange suppers, for people in town when they were sick or when someone passed away. Until she was in her seventies, she opened summer camps and cleaned and cooked for some of the wealthy people in the surrounding towns. Diligently, for years she was the janitor for the local Grange. Lugging water from home for the coffee and dishes, and starting the wood furnace for every meeting. For years she ran the Grange thrift shop, for the most part, by herself. Frequently, someone donated clothes that needed washing or mending before they could be sold. Nana would bring them home and fix them up, so the Grange could make money.

My grandmother never had a clothes dryer until a year before she died. Prior to this, she hung out the laundry for six people; on a clothes reel that was on a wooden platform off the back porch. I remember waking up in the middle of the night when I was little, scared because she wasn't in bed with me. Following the dim light, I could see through the house to the shed off the laundry room. I'd find her out there, wearing an apron over her bathrobe, hanging laundry out on the back porch. In the wintertime, by the time she got the other side of the reel the clothes would be frozen stiff, like there was a dead man in them. The tips of her poor thumbs and fingers were always wrapped in adhesive tape, because she worked so hard. The cracks in them were so deep that they'd be bleeding.

When I was about five years old, I started going to Grange meetings with her. I was the only child who was allowed to go upstairs in the hall and hear and see the secret work of the Grange meetings. You had to be thirteen to join. But, when I turned ten, they made a special exception for me. I had already been attending for years, helping Nana with suppers and running the thrift shop and coffee hour every Saturday. I loved being at the Grange almost as much as she did.

Saturday mornings some of the local ladies would come by to drink coffee and eat some of my grandmother's good cooking. They used to sit at one of the long tables out in the hall. They'd come in all dressed up; most of them would be wearing pretty fancy jewelry and good-sized diamond rings. Rarely did they buy any second-hand items from the thrift shop. Nana used to say, "No, they wouldn't buy anything here. They only come here to gossip." One Saturday morning, I was looking out the service window in the kitchen, just day dreaming, watching the ladies, wondering what it would be like if Nana and I could have all that nice stuff.

Feeling discouraged, I walked over to Nana, who was pouring an old agate kettle full of boiling into the sink to wash dishes. As I looked up into her tired old eyes behind her scratched eyeglasses, I said, "Nana, wouldn't you like to just sit around like those ladies, all dolled up and talking?" Without a moment's hesitation, she said, "You can't ring a hog that roots for a living. You have two hands, and you better learn how to use them, because no one in this life owes you a thing." Suddenly, in that moment, life for Nana and me seemed so hopeless. I didn't know whether to cry for myself or her. Instead, I wrapped my arms around her big belly covered with a heavily soiled apron, thinking, a Poor Nana, I love you.

To a Wild Rose

One Christmas when I was about five, I wanted more than anything to give my grandmother a present, something special, from just me. Christmas was and still is my favorite time of the year. Usually, I could talk Nana into letting me start decorating for Christmas right after Halloween! The older she got, the faster she gave in. In the late fall, when the big Sears and Spiegel Christmas catalogs came, Nana would let us kids pick out one special gift each. She never said anything, but, we wouldn't pick a real expensive gift. We knew she couldn't afford much. It was just wonderful to sit on the living room f loor and dream. I'd go through the catalogs over and over again.

Impatiently, I went on a mission to find something in that house to wrap up for Nana. It had to be new. My grandmother was the only mother I ever remembered having. I slept in her room with her until she died when I was sixteen. When I was little she'd rub my back and sing to me until I'd settled down and fallen asleep. Regularly, in the middle of the night, even in the summertime, she'd put socks on my icy cold feet. Years later, when I was in counseling, my doctor told me why my hands and feet were so cold. He said, "When the human body experiences trauma, and is in the fight-or-f light mode for extended periods of time, it takes the blood from your extremities, for the protection and survival of your vital organs."

Just as I was starting to get a little discouraged with my search, I spotted it. On the back of Nana's bureau, hidden behind a bunch of other stuff was a dusty, but brand-new box of To a Wild Rose powder from Avon. Running into the kitchen where she was cooking, I forced myself to sit down quietly at the table. After numbing around for a few minutes, I said, "Nana, are you going to use that box of To a Wild Rose powder that's on your bureau?" Cheerfully, she said, "No. Would you like it?"As I ran out of the kitchen yelling "I can have it, I can really have it!" Quickly, I went into her room and grabbed it. Then I crawled under the dining room table to wrap it, so she wouldn't see me.

Christmas mornings are the fondest memories I have of living with Nana. This one was the best. It was about giving her my gift. As she opened it, my hands were squeezed into tight fists on both sides of my face. I looked like I was going to explode! As she removed the last piece of wrapping paper, looking genuinely surprised,, an expression I rarely saw over the years, she said, "To a Wild Rose powder! How did you know, baby doll, that I needed some?" To use one of her expressions, "I felt like a million dollars, only half spent."

Many years later, when she was gone, I reflected back on that Christmas morning. An aching in my heart consumed me when I thought of her and the hard life she'd lived. My eyes welled up with tears. This Christmas memory was one of many which caused me to grieve the loss of my grandmother many times over. Years later, I would understand how resentment, anger, and fear were directly related to the feelings of rejection and abandonment that affected most of my family.

Lessons Came Hard and Nana Meant Business When She Taught Them

Predictably, there were many life lessons Nana made sure we learned. One of her biggest concerns was for us to know everything there was to know about personal hygiene. I can hear her now: "Water is free and soap doesn't cost that much. There's no need for anyone to be dirty!" Religiously, twice a day we were sent into the bathroom to take a good sponge bath. And we had better come out clean. If not, she would give us bath that we wouldn't soon forget.

The well at our house was shallow and down over a hill. Like clockwork, we could count on it going dry every year between early summer and early fall. We'd haul our drinking, cooking, and sponge-bath water in plastic milk jugs from Aunt Charlotte's house over town. When the water had served its original purpose, we'd use what little life it had left to flush the toilet. And we didn't want to get caught wasting water.

Usually, when the weather was warm enough, after supper we'd put on our bathing suits, grab a bar of soap, a towel, and a washcloth and head to the lake in the next town over to take a bath. Rarely, did we go to the river in town, because too many people would see us. And back then, a lot of the wastewater ran into the river from the old tannery. During the summer months, when a heavy rain storm was passing through, we'd put our bathing suits on and go under the eaves to wash, saving Nana the trip up to the lake.

I liked rain storms the best, because, after the storm passed, God always put the biggest and brightest rainbows across the sky in Lords Hill. I've never seen rainbows anywhere like the ones we used to have there. They would stretch from Nana's house to the ball field next door, then from the cemetery across the street, to over town and back.

I had learned in Sunday school, between crying spells, that rainbows are a symbol of God's love from Heaven. I always wanted to feel loved. Longingly, every time it rained, I hoped for a rainbow. There were two things I really loved about Sunday and Vacation Bible School: the chocolate sandwich cookies and grape Kool-Aid that they served on a big stone that covered the well, and making rainbows and necklaces out of macaroni. I especially liked gluing and painting. Anxiously, at the end of the day I'd be looking for the little blue bus that took us home. Attending church for a couple of hours was a big deal for me. Throughout my childhood I had a lot anxiety when Nana was out of my sight. Some of the ladies in town and at the church would either laugh at or get put out with me, because I would cry for my grandmother. Many of them had no idea what my home life was like. With the exception of Miss Loretta and Miss Polly, it seemed like no one really cared.

Confusing and unpredictable at best was my grandmother's love. When she loved me, I felt safe and couldn't imagine my life without her. When she was mad at me, her razor sharp tongue and aggressive actions were so unmerciful that by the time she got done, I'd wish you were dead. Townspeople as well as the teachers at school were aware of her harsh nature. One morning at the local store, a man she'd known for years was shooting off his mouth at the lunch counter. Standing by the cash register and listening for a few minutes, in front of God and everybody in that store, Nana blurted out, "If I bought that fool for what he knows and sold him for what he thinks he knows, I'd be a millionaire!"

My grandmother liked most of the people in Lords Hill. Close friends and many of the adults in town called her Nana. Immediately, I'd cringe when someone I knew she didn't like would ask, "Nana, don't you like me?" or "What's your opinion?" I used to think to myself, "Heaven help them," and I'd start looking for a rug somewhere to crawl under. Regularly when we were teenagers and she came into town, looking for us to come home, you could hear her blowing the horn and hollering our names out the car window from one block to another. She drove the same way day or night, with the pedal to the metal, either in the middle or on whatever side of the road she felt like driving on.

Occasionally local and state police would pull her over or she'd make them chase her all the way home. The minute they'd start to say something to her, she'd say, "Now you listen here, I pay taxes in this blasted town, and so-and-so does such-and-such, and I'll drive anywhere and any way I want to." If they pulled in the driveway behind her, she'd say, "What are you going to do to me now? I'm in my own yard." Hopelessly they'd respond, "Mrs. Hammond, please slow down," and they'd just shake their heads as they walked back to the cruiser. Invariably, she made short work out of standing her ground and telling people off. It wouldn't do a person any good to be thin-skinned around Nana. Anyone who was thin – skinned would be torn up and bleeding all the time!

CHAPTER 3

Martyrs, Tyrants, and Withering Vines

Throughout my childhood and teenaged years when I lived with Nana Hammond, our uncle Henry terrorized everyone in the house constantly. He had no regard for our fears or emotional pain. When we dared to express them, it only fueled his anger. We never knew when he was going to go on one of his random killing sprees of our pets. Nothing was safe or sacred with him. Sometimes he killed them in front of us, but most of the time he did it out in the garage. Occasionally when he was feeling extra cruel, he would make my grandmother cook the animals and we'd all have to eat some, while he looked on in a drunken rage.

There were three animals in particular that I have never been able to erase from my mind. One was my middle sister's pet rabbit, Love. He made Nana cook it, and we all had to eat some.

Desperately my sister cried to make him stop and my grandmother told her;

to shut-up! My older sister had a tricolor female kitten named, Colors. She worked really hard the summer she got this kitten. Proudly, she paid to have it taken care of at the vet's. She adored it. Sadly, my poor older sister had it worse than the rest of us. I was quite a bit younger than her, but I remember feeling really happy because she finally had something to love that would love her back and not hurt her. One afternoon with no warning at all, our uncle came out on the porch where we were sitting quietly, picked the cat up from the middle of the f loor where it was playing, and asked my sister, if she loved it? Immediately, without another word, he snapped its neck with one hand and dropped it back on the f loor.

The worst killing Uncle Henry did in front of us was my brother Jim's pony, Trigger. There was a big cement slab in front of the barn. Trigger was tied to the barn door. It was pouring freezing rain. Poor Trigger couldn't keep his legs under him, because it was so slippery. My uncle started hollering at him, the madder he got, the more Trigger slipped. When a bullwhip didn't make him stand, my uncle picked up a pitchfork and started stabbing him in the back end. In horror we all looked from the porch door and windows, screaming and crying.

Frequently we were his targets. Whenever we were sick with a cold or the f lu, if he was in the room or within earshot if we coughed, sneezed, or blew our nose, he would get in our faces. Gritting his teeth and spitting on us, he would say, "I'm going to kill you. You're doing on my thoughts." If you were sick, you had better have a pillow handy to muffle any noises you might make. Incredibly, the fear he put you in was far worse than the illness you had.

We had to lock our bedroom doors every night with deadbolts; if we made the terrible mistake of forgetting to lock the door, we'd wake up to him standing over us. Either he'd be glaring in our face with a wild and desperate look in his eyes, or he'd be muttering in a low voice about how he was going to slit our throats and gut us like a deer or crush our skulls in. Usually, he would have in his hand a knife, a gun, or a cane that he'd made out of a lead pipe.

At least seven times that I can remember, in the thirteen and a half years that I lived with Nana, he was taken to the state mental hospital in Concord, New Hampshire. Usually, it was after we were forced into Nana's bedroom for a few days. When we hadn't been seen for a few days, someone in the family would get worried. Most of the time, it would be Aunt Charlotte who called the state police. The lockdowns in Nana's bedroom were frightful. If we cried or made a noise, sometimes it was because we were hungry and had nothing to eat, Nana would slap us and say, "Hark, you miserable no good brat—he's going to hear you!"

Thankfully, she kept a commercial-sized metal vegetable can under the head of her bed that we used when we needed to go to the bathroom. The part I hated the most about this: we all had to wipe ourselves on the same rags, which Nana kept wrapped up under her pillow.

Intermittently, Uncle Henry would put himself in a lockdown upstairs in his bedroom, one time for six months. Nana would have us bring his food up to the top of the stairs and leave it on the floor outside his bedroom door. I felt like I was feeding a wild dog or a prisoner. Coming down the stairs, you could hear him start to slide the first of the three deadbolts on his door. Commonly, the small attic off his bedroom became his bathroom.

When he wasn't in a self-imposed lockdown, every day that I can remember through those nightmarish years; he'd play his TV and radio twenty-four hours a day, seven day a week. He'd have both of them blaring at the same time. Other times, when he wasn't sleeping, he would pound his feet on the floor for hours on end. Rhythmically, like he was doing an Indian war dance. His room was located directly over the kitchen. Nana used to worry that he'd come down through the ceiling. Occasionally, he'd start hollering and let out blood-curdling screams that would send chills through your body.

He refused to face anyone from the outside world, unless he was drunk. He would run upstairs and hide the minute someone pulled into the door yard. The few friends I did have, never came over to play. No birthday parties: if we did, he'd make us suffer for it after our visitors were gone. There were only few kids that dared to come to our house. Usually, they were our cousins. The majority of the kids in town wouldn't come near our house. Uncle Henry and the house were the talk of the town. They were too afraid that they wouldn't come out alive.

The Pathetic Side of Tyranny

There was one time when Uncle Henry locked himself in, that he demanded half gallons of ice cream at a time. Without fail, after he ate what he wanted, he'd let the rest melt on top of the bureaus. Once after the police had taken him away, we went to clean his room, only to find a pair of pliers and a bunch of his teeth stuck in layers of gooey ice cream on the top of his dresser. This was the time when the police wouldn't take him until Nana cleaned him up and cut his hair.

I can still see him sitting in a chair in the middle of the kitchen f loor. Involuntarily, in about three inch intervals, his legs and hands were jumping up and down, up and down. His hair had grown down into his eyes. The bridge of his nose was caked with dead skin and dandruff. His toenails and fingernails were so long they had curled and were starting to grow into his skin. The soles of his feet were blistered where he had burned them; insisting that the devil had come out through them. I scurried back and forth to the bathroom tub to fill a basin with hot water so Nana could clean him up. I remember how distressed she was, pleading with him as she fought back tears, "Henry, please sit still." I sobbed so hard all I could do was shake.

That same day, at the break of dawn, my brother Jim and I had to bury the little dog Uncle Henry had wired to a pile of trash and burned in the back yard in the middle of the night. I was about ten. I can still see tears of rage running down Jim's face, as he shoveled that little dog into the wheelbarrow. Frantically, he ran as fast as he could to the back of the house and up the hill to bury it. I had all I could do to keep up with him. Desperately, I ran as fast as I could to keep up. I loved my brother Jim more than anyone else in this world. I just couldn't bear to see him to do it alone.

Within a month or two, three at the most, after Uncle Henry had been taken away to the state hospital, he'd start calling Nana. Crying and begging, asking to come home, he'd promise that he would stay on his medication and not drink. Desperately pleading with Nana, and balling our eyes out, the minute my siblings and I heard of his possible return. To please, not let him come home. With a stoic look on her face, she'd show us no empathy at all. It wasn't uncommon for it to take days before she would answer us. Then she'd say, "I can't leave him there; he's my son. I have to let him come home." Usually his promises didn't last thirty days.

The truth of the matter was we cried partly because of his return. We also cried because of the false guilt that she made us feel, because we weren't saddened by his absence. Surprisingly, there were brief moments during the years when we lived with Uncle Henry when goodness would seep through from this very sick and sorrowful man.

When the first heavy snow of winter fell; Uncle Henry would make snow ice cream for us. To catch the fresh soft snow, we'd put big bowls out on the doorstep. After the bowls were full we'd hurry them inside. Immediately, Uncle Henry added evaporated milk, sugar, and vanilla extract. He'd mix it quickly, because the snow melted so fast. Quickly, he'd spoon it into plastic containers and freeze it for about a half hour. It was yummy. I can still see the big smiles on all our faces. If only for a brief moment in time, Uncle Henry was not hurting us, himself, or our animals. Occasionally, in the late summer or early fall, for another treat, he would make us the best homemade French fries and onion rings I've ever had.

Ironically, the sad truth about this poor man was that one of his many personalities was extremely book smart. On the rare occasion when the household was stable enough for us to do some homework, he could help you solve any math problem or answer any history question there was. The times when he wasn't feeling awfully mean, he would hang an old saddle from the rafters in the barn so my sisters and I could pretend that we had a horse to ride. Beaming with pride, he would stand there and watch us play for a few minutes. I always felt sad as he walked away, because I knew our fun and safe time together would soon be over.

When we were little if we had a hard time losing a baby tooth, especially me, Uncle Henry would tie a piece of thin string around the tooth and the other end to a door knob. Then he'd slam the door, and bingo, the tooth was out! Today that would probably be considered traumatic. In comparison to the other stuff we were living through, I was actually grateful for his help. I had a lot of problems with my teeth, so I was always choking. It seems no matter how hard I tried to hate Uncle Henry, I just couldn't. Today, I know it's because God didn't want me to. I didn't understand this as a child. Today, I am grateful I didn't!

Fantasies Are Just That—Fantasies

During my early years with Nana, until I was about eleven years old, I lived and played in a fantasy world. Between hating myself and wishing I were dead like my mother, I spent hours pretending that I was a teacher with students. I was someone important, and people wanted to listen to me. I was always kind and good to my make-believe students. When they didn't behave, I calmly spoke to them. But I never punished them the way I had been. Nana had given me unlimited access to the horse hair–plaster walls in the front hall. Freely I could write on them with chalk, pencils, and pens. It not only kept me entertained, but also out of her hair !

Once when Uncle Henry was away at the state hospital, I went rummaging in the attic off his bedroom. I found an old white leather-bound Bible. I would open the front hall door that faced the cemetery across the street and pretend that all the people over there were real. I'd open the Bible and make believe I was reading. I was a preacher who was telling them about God. It was only in my make-believe life that I had any life at all. It was the only time when my Aunt Charlotte couldn't tell me that I didn't hear, see, or feel what I had heard, seen, or felt.

The hours I didn't spend "preaching" in the front hall, I lay on the couch, staring at a picture of my mother that hung on the wall. I would desperately try to remember seeing her face when she was alive, but to no avail. My mind was void of any memory of her at all. Other times I was across the street at her grave. I was about six when I started to climb the stone wall at the edge of the cemetery where there was a direct route to my mother's grave. Until I was about eleven, I spent hours crying and begging God to bring her back as I glared through swollen eyes at the sky and our house across the street. I would try to bargain with Him to bring her back.

I would promise Him everything—that I'd never be naughty again or that He could punish me any way He wanted to—if only I could have my mother. For a fleeting moment, I'd stop sobbing and fall into the fantasy that my dad cared about me and was coming to get me. I'd pretend to see his truck driving by the cemetery as he looked for me, but no truck ever came. Then I would go back to crying so hard I felt like my bones would crack.

The year before I turned twelve, I was like little Jackie Paper in one of my favorite songs, "Puff the Magic Dragon." I no longer returned to the front hall to pretend, and all the fantasies I'd once had about God returning my mother died a sudden death. I had lived the first eleven of my formative years with people who were out of control and extremely codependent, and I was too. In order to feel some sort of love and acceptance, I became a caregiver to my abusers. I took total responsibility for the things they said and did and their happiness. The hate I felt for myself grew all the time, because every day I was becoming more like them.

With Uncle Henry's craziness, my grandmother's need to be a raging martyr, and Aunt Charlotte's using me as a pawn in her twisted adultery game, I began an unconscious and dramatic separation from my child self. I spent the next four years in Lords Hill with Nana and Uncle Henry and the last two with Aunt Charlotte, after my grandmother died. Those years were laden with anger and the onset of addictions, my free will gone wild.

CHAPTER 4

School Days Filled with Humiliation and Shame

My school years were horrible. Kindergarten through sixth grade I cried every day, usually until I hyperventilated and started choking. The intense separation anxiety I experienced when I was away from my grandmother was extreme. I was an emotional wreck. In first grade our family doctor put me on Donnatal Phenobarbital Elixir, to calm me down and help me tolerate school. Throughout these years, the teachers often kept me isolated from the rest of the class. Usually with a three-sided moveable partition, because my crying spells were so disruptive. Often I sat in either the principal's or guidance counselor's office, trying to do my school work. When I wasn't going through trauma at home, I was bullied and picked on at school and on the bus ride between home and school.

First grade was the only time I remember feeling special or wanted by my teachers. Little did I know, the motivation behind my sudden popularity was the plan they had for me in the Christmas pageant. In late November, we started practicing Christmas songs. One of the songs was "All I Want for Christmas is My Two Front Teeth." I had lost my two front teeth in September. Out of all the kids in my class wasn't I the only one missing two front teeth! Suddenly, the teachers had time to pay attention to me, coaching me on the platform in front of the whole class as I sang, "All I Want for Christmas is My Two Front Teeth." And sing I did. My brother Jim taught me how to whistle when I was about four, so whistling through my front teeth was easy.

I was a neurotic little girl, on medication, displayed in front of a room full of mostly strangers, performing solo, no less! The day of the play, the adults laughed as if they were making fun of me instead of thinking I was cute or talented. I was horrified through the whole ordeal. At times I felt like I was going to collapse in front of all the strange faces smirking at me; I felt sick and hot. I kept watching the door that went out to the hallway, hoping my dad would show up, but he never did. That day still haunts me.

That fall, I had sent my dad one of my school papers. It had special stars on it and a good grade. We rarely saw him, so Nana helped me send it to him through the mail. When I went to drop off his Christmas present that year as usual I stepped inside the door and waited against the wall like a stranger while he opened his gift. His third wife and her kids sat around the table or stood in a hallway off the kitchen, staring at me like I was some kind of freak. I was nervous because no one talked to me, and my father said very little. Suddenly, I blurted out, "Dad, did you get my paper?" His wife, all her kids, and my dad burst into laughter. He said, "Yeah—you mean the one written on wide-ruled yellow paper, done with a fat pencil? I got it." Every time I tried to get my father to care about me, it always destroyed more of my self-esteem.

The kids at school used to call me terrible names and make fun of me for being a cry-baby. Some of them would terrorize me by repeating horrible things they'd heard their parents say about my mother and father. I didn't know how to defend myself; I didn't really know either of my parents, so I started lashing out by cursing and swearing back at them. Then I'd get punished, and lose my recess. Or I'd be put into the hall corner with my desk, while the rest of the class enjoyed a holiday party or crafts. Sometimes, they would get put me in the supply closet upstairs. I can remember sitting in the closet peering out a little dirty window right next to the rope that rang the school bell. I used to be tempted to ring that bell, but I didn't. Occasionally, the first-grade teacher, who tried to like me, would let me ring it if I was in there when it was time for recess or to go home.

The fall I was in third grade, one of Aunt Charlotte's sons made me a fairy godmother costume for Halloween. I was very excited. And after the parade that night, some of the mothers in town were having a contest at the annual Halloween party at the Odd Fellows Hall. That day at school, a couple of kids in my class told me at recess that their mother said, that my real father was this man in town who was a wealthy womanizer and heavy drinker. That's why I didn't see my father, because he wasn't my real father at all. And my mother was nothing but a trollop when she was alive. I started to curse, scream, and cry to the high heavens. Guess who got punished in school that afternoon?

As fate would have it, for whatever reason, Nana decided to come into the little red schoolhouse that day and wait for me in the hall. She was usually too tired to climb the stairs to come in. She had started to have gout in her right leg that morning. I was anxious and worried about her before I left home and begged her not make me go to school. She assured me that she'd be okay and reminded me that I didn't want to miss the Halloween party at school with all the other kids.

Nana tended to have an intuition about things, which is probably why she climbed the schoolhouse stairs that day. There I was in the corner of the hall at my desk, sobbing my eyes out. I told Nana what happened. When she got through with that teacher, let's just say, "I'm still surprised, there is a roof left on that schoolhouse. God Himself would have had to strike her dead to stop her." By suppertime that night her leg was swollen to twice

35

its size. I was afraid of the kids who had picked on me, so I didn't want to march in the parade or go to the party the hall. She said, "You are going to that parade, and no miserable puke in this town or their kids are going to stop you!"

I marched in the parade that night, and to make sure that no one bothered me. Nana drove her old Buick slow beside me all the way through town. She used a cane to climb the stairs to get inside the Odd Fellows Hall. She sat off to the side while I bobbed for apples and ate donuts dangling from string, just like the other kids. My grandmother was the only parent there who wasn't helping to put the party on. When they announced the winners for the three best costumes, I took third place. The biggest newspaper around was there that night covering the party. The next afternoon, wasn't I on the front page with the other winners.

I cried my eyes out when we got home, because I thought Nana was going to die. I would be to blame because she was so upset over me at school that day. We got ready for bed. As sick as she was and as big as I was, she had me climb onto her lap in the living room rocking chair because I was so distraught. She said, "Don't worry about it, baby doll. I'm not going to die." I clung to her neck. I can still smell the hot tea she'd been drinking on her breath; and the Dip pity-Do hair gel that she used every day to comb her scarcely gray hair into a wave.

The Bullies Got Bigger

Over the years, the verbal abuse of school bullies became physical torment. I had gum and lollipops stuck in my hair, and spit balls thrown at me. In high school I was shoved down a flight of stairs. One boy in particular stole my lunch and ate it in front of me every day. When I finally dared to say something, I ended up flat on my back in the middle of the gym floor with a cracked elbow. For fear of their own safety, no one dared to help me, so they just stood by and watched.

It seemed the only connections I could make in high school, were with kids who were troubled. Most days I skipped school and smoked marijuana and drank booze in someone's barn until the bus came to bring me home. A few times I did hallucinogenic drugs, like acid, and opium. I just didn't care what happened to me or what I did.

One year in junior high, some older kids who were part of the "in crowd" pretended to like me. And said, They wanted to be my friends. They got me really drunk so I would go to the local store and steal cigarettes for them. I did it. Then they fed me a couple more black Russians. Then they started telling me I was thief and they didn't trust me. They got in my face and laughed at me.

The next thing I knew, I was laying in the back seat of a car in the dead of winter, with frozen puke all over me. I was so drunk I was paralyzed. I could barely open my eyes. Through a window, I could see all of them partying in some house. The next thing I knew, I was lying against the guard rail on the side of a major road. They thought I was going to die, so they threw me out. I still don't know who picked me up or remember the ride back to Lords Hill. Then in a daze barely able to stand, I was taking a a hot shower. Holding me up was a woman from town and her boyfriend. They were trying to save my life. I had babysat quite often for this woman over the years and she never used me wrong. But, her home had quite a reputation as a party house where anything would go.

While she washed and dried my clothes, I sat at the kitchen table in her pajamas, trembling all over and drinking hot coffee. She told me, "I'm sorry, but as soon as it's light out, you are going to have to walk home. I don't want Nana to think you've been here." Her house was about a mile over the bridge into

Maine. I was still so intoxicated I don't remember the walk home, only staggering across the bridge. It was no less than a divine intervention that I didn't die on the side of the road that night.

Most of my bullies had followed me from first grade to high school. I had no solace from anyone anywhere. I felt destined to live in unending terror, and I was! Mr. Thompson, the school guidance counselor, was my only saving grace during those years. From middle school through the first one and a half years I attended high school, I saw him almost every day. I loved Mr. Thompson; he seemed like the only person who listened to me and really cared about my pain.

In the 70s, teachers were still allowed to smoke in the school. I can see Mr. Thompson now, taking some pretty heavy drags off his cigarettes. His dark, bushy eyebrows seemed to meet in the middle of his nose when he was uncomfortable with what I was saying. I had started expressing myself like everyone else in my family, swearing and ranting when I was upset.

Mr. Thompson never reported the things I told him about what was going on in our home. Nana met with him a few times. I remember seeing her through the window in his room, crying her eyes out. I believe the poor man didn't know what to do about the whole situation. I'm sure he didn't want to hurt this poor old woman, who was doing the only thing she knew how at the time. Otherwise we would have become wards of the state and might have ended up even worse off.

Mr. Thompson stayed faithful to me as long as I was in school. He was the only real friend I had during those difficult years. After I was married and had children, Mr. Thompson and I stayed in touch at least once a year. When Aunt Charlotte saw his obituary in the newspaper, she called me right away. She knew what he meant to me and that I would want to attend his funeral.

Mr. Thompson had dedicated so much of himself to the kids at school over the years. During the summer months he owned and operated a business in an ocean-side community in Maine. I was sure there would be a glorious celebration honoring him, with hundreds of people from miles around. A mere handful of immediate family members were there, and maybe three other people besides me. I sobbed from the beginning to the end of his funeral service.

Driving home that day, I felt punch drunk. I was crying so hard, I couldn't see anything in front of or around me. I kept chanting out loud, "How can this be? He was such a good man." I felt sickened and crushed on his behalf at the mere handful of people who came to pay their respects for this man. As long as I have a memory, I will always be grateful for the safe haven he provided for me all those hours, days, and years so long ago.

Losing Heart and Drowning in Shame

By the time we were four or five, one of Aunt Charlotte's family members started encouraging us to smoke and drink alcohol. When I was twelve years old, I was smoking and drinking on a regular basis. I make no excuses for myself today: but back in the early stages of my life, things always moved fast, and lessons I learned were hard at best. In truth, I was acting like the animals in the only jungle I had ever known.

I am not proud of the mistakes I made during my teenage and young adult years. Every day that I live the reality of where I've been and what I've done is only a thought away. These memories serve to keep me humble, lest I get a big ego, become full of pride, and forget where I've been. It is my prayer that others will be able to see that it doesn't matter how lost and far down any human being can go. There's hope. I've lost track of the number of times God has stepped in and literally saved my life.

Years ago I was filled with feelings of anger, abandonment, and rejection. I had an attitude of "Bring it on! Try me on for size," even with God. My life growing up fostered these feelings and attitudes. The good news is, through those dark days, I have come to realize, God is full of mercy and grace. And the difference is this: mercy withholds from us what we deserve, and grace gives us what we don't deserve.

At thirteen I started stealing alcohol from Aunt Charlotte's cellar and money from her purse. I took full advantage of her being drunk and not paying attention. I had learned how to work her, like she'd worked me. Nana was getting older, more tired and sicker than I realized. I started to fight as well when it came to others controlling me. I was getting older and our positions were changing. I seized every moment that I triumphantly held my ground.

In my opinion, the perception a lot of adults, professionals, and some "godly people" have about children and young adults who turn to stealing, is baloney! People often think they steal because they're thieves or some kind of bad seed that will never bear good fruit. I can't speak for the rest of the world, but I was not destined to be a thief, nor did I enjoy stealing. I was as nervous as a cat on a hot tin roof when I was doing it. I knew if I got caught, I was dead on the spot. Nana and Aunt Charlotte had their shortcomings, to be sure, but stealing was not one of them.

I believe stealing, just like any other nasty habits, quirks, addictions, or codependency issues, is part of the fallout that comes with an abusive and traumatic childhood. Stealing as a child and teenager was nothing more and nothing less than something I did for a feeling of satisfaction, restitution, and control. Stealing caused a chemical release in my brain, like a cigarette, alcohol, or a good old-fashioned sugary drunk. Thanks to God, stealing was one of the many compulsive struggles that I didn't become hooked on for years.

I had an experience in my late thirties that supports this theory. I felt convicted to pursue a volunteer position, I knew God had made me hungry for—working with abused children who for the most part been permanently removed from their homes and families. They were awaiting their unknown futures in an orphanage. The most grievous part of my short-lived volunteer experience was that the orphanage was supported by a religious institution. I had naively thought that a Christian based refuge for these children would have been a little more compassionate. I'm not saying they were mean, but, as far as I was concerned, the Jesus that I had come to know would not have viewed these orphaned children the same way these religious people did.

The children and I were like kindred spirits; we connected immediately. Most of them were under the age of twelve and had already lived lives of untold abuse and horror. One evening I was strictly warned about these young children. I was told; not to trust them, because they would manipulate me and my love. And I should watch my pocketbook, because they would steal from me the first chance they got. My heart sank, and my jaw dropped to f loor as I looked at the woman telling me this. I felt like saying, "How on this side of life can you rationalize seeing these victimized children in the same light as the perpetrators who got them here?" Instead I said, "Are you serious?" She responded in an indignant tone, "You don't understand!" I replied, "Oh no, *you* don't understand. I understand all too well!"

Suffice it to say when I left that evening I was not welcome to return. I am deeply saddened by people who have not had to endure loss and abuse as a child, because they seem to have a lot of misconceptions about what motivates abused children or makes them tick. It's like amputating a broken soul that just needs a little love and some mending. I know the agony of my childhood caused most of the acting out I did well into my twenties.

As I got older, when Nana went to discipline me, I would start swearing at her and telling her she wasn't my real mother. Sick with grief afterwards, I apologized, because I never wanted to hurt her in any way. She'd always respond, "You wouldn't have said it if you hadn't meant it." The hard part was I really did love her, but my pain was greater than anyone or anything else in my life. I was giving what I had gotten. And I suffered either way.

By the time I was thirteen I was running the streets when and where I wanted. The era of being stuck all summer in a hot laundry-mat where Nana worked until two years before she died, doing laundry for kids from wealthy New York families, was over. I was finished watching privileged kids ride the horses at the stable in back of the laundry-mat. We would be boiling hot while they got swimming lessons at the lake. We didn't have two cents to rub together; but they had money to buy gum, candy, and chips at the canteen at the top of the hill. When I used to help Nana with their laundry, I still remember being brought to a dreamy place where I have never lived, by the delicate aroma of expensive perfume that filled their clothes. And the Juicy Fruit gum wrappers I'd find, still carried a sweet smell.

The laundry workers weren't allowed to eat in the food hall, "up top," as it was called. Instead we ate in a makeshift kitchen that Nana had fashioned in a small entryway behind the big washing machines with a door leading to a path behind the horse stalls. The dirty laundry water would flow through a big ditch in the cement floor that ran under the stools we sat on. If we were lucky, after all the summer kids ate their lunch, the cook "up top" would give us some of the leftover hot food; and a big jug of pink lemonade that the rich kids called bug juice. Nana always made it clear that we might get some and we might not. "So don't fuss if there aint any," she used to say.

As tired and worry-worn as she looked every day, Nana worked at this summer camp and around home, until she just couldn't push anymore. She used said, "If it's the last thing I do, I won't have my name in the town report for unpaid taxes next year." My grandmother had a lot of pride when it came to paying her bills. She wouldn't cheat a soul, even if her life was to depend it on. She was a firm believer in people earning their salt and paying their way.

When the camp owners from New York paid Nana her first allotment of money halfway through the season, she'd take one or two of us at a time to a little establishment out on the main road across from the state park. It had a grill, a soda fountain, and a game room—and a lot of candy counters. And a small selection of cigarettes that were popular at the time. If we had at least tried to be good and helped to fold the laundry; going there was one of our special treats for the summer. Then in the fall, Nana and Aunt Charlotte would always make sure we went to the two local fairs.

Aunt Charlotte worked at the camp with Nana for many years, but she usually kept herself occupied by having sex with the man who owned the horses and ran the stable out back. When she wasn't with him, she was giving rich young men from New York their first kisses. I used to curl up and hide on a stack of damp laundry bags, under a long bench in a big storage area to stay out of the way. In front of it, Nana and my two older siblings stood at a bench and folded the laundry. Nana would be ranting about Aunt Charlotte not being around to do her share of the work and taking off to be a no-good tramp. Sometimes I felt so anxious and overwhelmed I would tune everyone out; then I could hear only the banging and vibrations from the big washers and extractors until they lulled me off to sleep.

The best thing that happened to me the year I turned thirteen was that I was accepted into a work program at the high school that Mr. Thompson had told me about. It was called the Cedar Program; low-income, often troubled kids were the only ones eligible to work for it. I worked for the program for two summers. It was actually the only time that I liked being at school.

The janitor, Mr. Marshfield, was a kind man who took me under his wing and treated me with respect. We had a lot of laughs together while the other kids and I dug everything from gum to boogers off the undersides of the school desks. Graphite removal was my favorite because I loved having a paint brush in my hands. Mr. Marshfield wasn't so keen about it, because I painted like I talked, a hundred miles an hour, and as Nana used to say, " jumping around like a fart in a skillet!"

I had two other saving graces during my teenage and adult years, Aunt Eddie and Aunt Geneva. They had both been married to two of my mother's older brothers. Aunt Eddie used to babysit sometimes while Nana worked, but it wasn't until my early twenties we became close. I was especially close to Aunt Geneva during my childhood and through my early twenties, until she died of cancer. Aunt Geneva never had a good relationship with our family and wanted as little to do with them as possible. She wasn't any bigger than a minute in stature, but she was a stick of dynamite when you crossed her. A lot of people in town and in my family had run-ins with her. She and I never had a falling out. She loved me and was better to me than most of my own family.

Sometimes I would go to her house to hide from Aunt Charlotte. I remember one time Aunt Charlotte pounded on Aunt Geneva's front door, thinking she was going to bully her into making me leave. Aunt Geneva let her have her say, and then refused to tell her whether I was there or not. A few minutes later, after Aunt Geneva had stewed on it, she marched all four feet and ten inches of herself up the street past the general store, with a lit cigarette in her hand, right to Aunt Charlotte's front door.

I followed a ways back behind Aunt Geneva; I didn't want to cause her any trouble for helping me. Standing on the door step, nose to chest with Aunt Charlotte, Aunt Geneva informed her that anytime I wanted to go to her house to hide or stay, I could, and she'd let me. And no drunken so and so, who didn't have a leg to stand on; when it came to talking about anyone else, was going to tell her otherwise! Aunt Charlotte never opened her mouth. I decided to stay. Aunt Geneva looked at me and said, "You do what you want, but if she puts her hands on you, come and see me." I don't remember Aunt Charlotte uttering one word to me.

If anything, my home life got worse. Uncle Henry was as crazy as ever. My brother Jim and he were now getting into physical fights. One day Jim and I came home from over town, as we were walking up the cement steps, we saw Nana in a chair on the porch. Uncle Henry was pulling her head back, holding Jim's hunting knife to her throat. Jim wrestled him to the floor. Nana and I stood by screaming as my brother put the knife against Henry's throat. He never bothered Jim again.

When he'd go on one of his bad drinking binges, Uncle Henry seemed to be getting braver. He made friends, more or less, with a crazy drunk who lived a couple of streets away from our house. Uncle Henry and this guy would be liquored up by mid afternoon; they'd hitch Chico, my uncle's old paint horse to the wagon with a lantern hanging from the buggy and ride for miles around, drinking.

Hours later, well into the night, the police would come to Nana's, usually about three or four o'clock in the morning. Uncle Henry and his drinking pal had either disturbed the peace by terrorizing people or were turned in for being drunk and abusing Chico. They would be in the county jail, cooling off and sobering up. We would get out of bed to go with Nana to bring the wagon and Chico home. We'd tie baling twine to his halter to the front door handle of the car, and Nana would patiently drive less than five miles per hour. We were all crying because my uncle had beat Chico badly and had run him ragged. He'd be foaming at the mouth. His poor feet and legs were so tired that they'd cross over each other when he walked, barely holding him up. Things just seem to keep going from bad to worse.

Aunt Charlotte became physically more ill, yet, she wouldn't let go of her lifestyle. She was always controlling Nana's relationships with her other children and the way she thought we should live. My grandmother was crying all the time. My aunt was still meeting with her boyfriends, often having sex in a car right out in our driveway. We could hear her when we were trying to sleep. But Nana lied and covered up for her all the time. I'm not sure why or how she justified what her daughter was doing. All I know is, I hated it. It made me feel guilty and dirty for things I had no control over.

My two older sisters were hanging on by their shoestrings. My middle sister ran away from home when she was fourteen and never came back. My older sister was still living at home and being abused worse than the rest of us. If something was broken or went missing, she was blamed and beaten for it both physically and verbally. The things I remember my grandmother and Aunt Charlotte doing and saying to my older sister, I can barely forgive them for to this day. She had no self-esteem at all and wasn't a fighter like the other three of us. She ended up married to the first guy who came along and showed her any love at all. He was a nitwit. My grandmother, with all her "finesse" used to tell her, "You better not have any children with that fool. You'll be lucky if they come out all right!"

Surprisingly, I have a few good memories I treasure from that time in my life. One of my fondest was stepping off the school bus in the fall and standing at the end of the driveway smelling the piccalilli and mincemeat Nana would cook in big roaster ovens out on the front porch. As I approached the porch door, there'd be beads of fragrant steam streaming down the windows panes. Inside the kitchen there were always six or eight pies, still warm. I'd throw my school bag down and sit at the kitchen table. Warm mince pie was my favorite, and Nana would let me eat my fill, complemented by ice-cold milk.

Memories like this and the few other good ones, over the years, made me feel like it would have been easier if my childhood and teenage years had been all bad; without love or goodness. Then in some strange way, the hard stuff wouldn't have hurt so much.

CHAPTER 5

Confusion, Chaos, and Fear Reign

By the time I was fifteen I was looking for happiness and love in codependent relationships. I was making irreversible choices that would haunt me for years to come. Knowing in my head that God would forgive me through His Son, Jesus, was the easy part. It was the self hate and condemnation that would hold me hostage for years. I used to wish I could be like one of the little children on the Velcro board at Sunday school, sweet and innocent, looking at Him in awe, secure in the safety of pure love.

My life wasn't all bad; I did learn some valuable life skills while living with my grandmother that are still an asset to me today. However, school and book learning were never a priority in my family. Undeniably, hard work and common sense were necessities if we intended to survive.

The fact that my existence had been riddled with emotional, mental, and often physical abuse - not to mention loss, rejection, and abandonment - was never a topic to be discussed. Nor were they to be used for a reason or an excuse for anything I did wrong or failed at. It just was. It never failed to amaze me how some of my family members would do horrible things, often worse than other people in town: yet, they judged and talked about others like they had a handle on life and the right perspective on how people should live!

Between the age of thirteen and sixteen, my behaviors became more and more out of control with each passing day. The anxiety about losing Nana never abated. My defiance of Aunt Charlotte and her control over my life changed course. She was backing off a little. When she did come at me, it was more physical, so I avoided her as much as possible. When I was twelve, Aunt Charlotte had paid to have all my teeth, which my great-grandmother helped to ruin, fixed. So, every time she got mad at me she'd say, "I'd knock those f'in teeth out of your mouth if I didn't have so much money into them!"

The boys at school never showed any interest in me, so I hung around an older crowd. I met my first real boyfriend at a party in the same town my mother had died in twelve years earlier. He was nine years older than me, a great guy whose family had their own dysfunctional issues. However, he was a gem and treated me better than anyone else ever had. Nana loved him, which was a big plus, because most of the time she didn't like many of our friends.

My grandmother's philosophy was: "It's better to be an old man's darling than a young man's slave." Consequently, by the time I was fifteen, I was allowed to have a boyfriend with whom I was sexually active. I could have done so even younger if I had wanted to. Love was often an uncontrolled sexual action in our family. If you felt like acting on it, even if it was wrong, everyone just looked the other way like it wasn't happening.

A good example of this was when I went to work at a local lumber yard in my early twenties. Most of the men and women who worked there didn't know who I was related to. One of my mother's older brothers drove a tractor-trailer truck for them. And while he was still married to my Aunt Eddie, he ran around every chance he got with other women. One day when I was walking through a hallway, I passed by the office door of one of the senior owners of the company. I overheard him telling his nephew about my uncle and how that behavior ran in my uncle's family. He said that his mother and sister had always slept around too.

The family that owned the lumber company were nice people and very good to me. When the man who who had this, found out that I was crying and who I was related to, he came and apologized immediately. I couldn't help but forgive him right there on the spot. His eyes exhibited more empathy for what he had said, than any persons in my family ever had. Over the years I coined this theory and try to live by the reality of it to this day; the truth may hurt us, cause loss, and bring us happiness or even restitution. At times it might even cause untold pain and suffering, but the one thing you can NEVER take away from it is, "It's always fair!" If this man had been lying, well, shame on him. Unfortunately, his only sin was gossip and very few people that I know of have escaped that snare.

I personally never saw my grandmother act inappropriately. I did hear a lot of stories about her when I got older, after she was gone. Although it broke my heart and steadily toppled her from the pedestal I had always set her on, I couldn't at any point in my life deny or confirm whether there was any truth in any of these stories. Years later, I heard more talk and even some stories from my aunts and uncles before they died. Today I believe, her fate like everyone else', was and is, hers to answer to God for. Lest I fall f latter on my face than I already have.

A Little Too Late

The summer before Nana died, I would have to say that, "She tried to do something with me before it was too late, too late for what? I still don't really know, and I honestly don't think she did either." I was burned out from all the drama and trauma at school. In life-experience years, I had far surpassed all my peers, and the days of trying to fit in were only getting harder. Then one weekend it all came to a head with Nana and me. I was coming home drunk and defiant more often than not; finally she snapped on me one last time.

What started off as a screaming match in the dining room escalated into her chasing me around the dining room table; suddenly, I saw her pick up one of those heavy old green window shades that had fallen from the window. The hardware holding it up had broken and it was lying on the buffet table.

Without thinking, I ran to the bathroom at the other end of the house. I was trapped. There was no time to hook the lock on the door. I looked behind me as I climbed up onto the back of the tub; she was right there. I knew I was in for it, but good. As I stood pinned with my back against the wall, I had a hasty decision to make. I could have picked my foot up and tried to kick her away; had it been anyone else, yes, but not my grandmother. I couldn't have done it if my life depended on it. In some strange way, I knew I deserved the beating I was going to get. And I did. There were two sharp metal hooks on both ends of that window shade. By the time she got done beating me, I had some pretty good-sized welts and a few cuts worth noticing. I can hear her words just as if she were standing here today. "I'll make something out of you, if I draw my last breath and die trying to do it or you'll be no good just like your father!"

The next words out of my grandmother's mouth were, "Now you go to school tomorrow. You wear shorts, and you tell them where you got those marks and why. And I don't give a hoot if the state comes and takes you away. I'll have your bags all packed for them!" Here's the sad part: I wore shorts. No one ever asked what happened and I never said. Only my cousins knew it was Nana's handiwork, and they were just glad to be them and not me.

After this, one day I walked five and a half miles to one of the bordering towns; I had to find someone to help me make sense of how bad I'd been and why. I felt convicted to go to the parish house of the Catholic priest, Father Lampron. I knocked on his door. The minute this gentle, small-framed, gray-haired man opened the door, I burst into tears. "Can you please help me find God?" I cried. He invited me in. The rest is a blur. While talking to me, he was kind and good to me. Then lovingly, he sent me on my way with a Bible with many parts of scripture underlined for me to read. I still have the Bible and treasure it to this day.

It became more obvious over the years: Nana really didn't know how to straighten her own life out, never mind give us a better one. When I went into counseling in my mid-twenties, I had a lot of anger to sort through in regards to her choices and behaviors.

Headed to a Point of No Return

It was all par for the course, by the time I was fifteen; I was a full-blown drinker and cigarette smoker and occasional marijuana user. I looked older than I was. So, I was served in barrooms every weekend; the drinking age was twenty-one, and I could buy beer without having to show any form of ID in most of the stores in surrounding towns. I stayed over some nights at my boyfriend's house, but still slept with Nana when I was home. I quit school in the early spring of my tenth-grade year, when I was fifteen and a half years old. Nana signed for me to leave school and get working papers. Immediately, I went to work in a shoe shop a couple of towns away. An older woman in town, Edwina, a real hot ticket, worked at the same factory where I got a job. She'd pick me up at the end of our driveway every morning when it was still dark out.

Nana had a heart condition that was getting worse. She lost a lot weight. It seemed to me like overnight, the woman who was once robust and just shy of six feet tall, with a strong

Constitution, with swift and productive hands was reduced to a frail creature who was become half of what she'd once been. The nights I stayed away from home were filled with more and more guilt. My brother Jim and I were the only two still living at home with Nana and Uncle Henry; so, Aunt Charlotte was always ranting and raving at us for leaving Nana, as sick as she was, home alone.

My grandmother had never talked to me about the facts of life, so when I started to menstruate at eleven years old; I thought God was punishing me for being bad and I was going to die like my mother. When I told Nana what was going on, she handled my new unwanted challenge simply and abruptly. Every month, I screamed, screeched, and swore that "I wouldn't have it and no one could make me!" Finally, one day she said, as she slapped me around a bit, "Listen here. You better get it through your head right now - there ain't a thing you're going to do about it. You're going to have it whether you like it or not!" She showed me one more time what to use and how, then she walked away. I threw a fit for about six months. And then life went on.

Looking back, I realize there was no way of knowing the sad and most unfortunate event that would happen next to me. This older and wonderful boyfriend had, bought me a diamond ring and a beautiful cedar chest that's a little worse for wear now, but still and will forever reside at the foot of my bed. It holds all that has been salvageable and precious to me over the years. Even the first Valentine card, I ever received from him. I ended up pregnant before my sixteenth birthday in October. I had taken myself to the family planning clinic and got on birth control, but between drinking and my home life, I forgot to take my pills a good part of the time.

My boyfriend, who was a great guy, was the father; he could see the unraveling of my life and Nana's health. Both he and Nana thought it best for me not to have the baby. I can't say even to this day what I felt. I didn't even know who I was. Nana took me to our family doctor, ironically the doctor who had delivered me. What I do remember, while at his office was feeling extreme embarrassment and shame. I just wanted to die, like I had wanted so many other times in my life. At almost five months pregnant, I was too far along for him to help me.

Immediately, I was sent to larger hospital where he had a connection. I would have an abortion that would be camouflaged as a D & C: dilation of the cervix, and curettage, the surgical scraping of part of the uterus lining and removal of its contents with vacuum aspiration. Two days before my sixteenth birthday, Nana took me at 5:00 a.m. and my boyfriend paid for it.

After I got home, I was shivering with cold and couldn't get warm. So, I did what we used to do as kids; I got the big blanket off the living room couch, lay over the register on the dining room floor, and had Nana turn up the heat. When the register started to blow hot air, the blanket would fill with hot air. I lay there, unconscious, for what seemed like an eternity. When I tried to get up I could barely move. The pain was so horrible. I was also hemorrhaging badly, too badly to stay home, so Nana called our family doctor. I was admitted to the hospital for three days and needed two blood transfusions before I could come home. The day before I left the hospital, Nana was admitted with congestive heart failure. She and I spent my sixteenth birthday in the hospital together, her in a hospital bed hooked up to tubes and me in a wheelchair, weak and sick.

Things between my boyfriend and me were forever changed. There was no turning back. Just like my immediate family, I grew crazier and more compulsive by the day. He started to withdraw. I could not seem to control my outbursts of anger or the crying jags that would last for hours and became increasingly worse every time I drank. He could no longer handle the way I was acting.

To this day, there are two things that I'm sure of in my heart, aside from the fact that I had undiagnosed PTSD (post-traumatic stress disorder) from my childhood. My boyfriend's sister, with whom he shared an apartment, had a lot to do with our separation. They were also trying to survive, because of their parents, the only way they knew how. His sister was controlling and very jealous like their mother. He paid most of the bills and would let her have everything her way to avoid any conflict. It didn't matter that she had several different boyfriends living with them. The bottom line was that she wanted her brother all to herself and if she couldn't, she'd throw hissy fits, like their mother. He had a good-paying job and a generous heart. He was an easy meal ticket for her, and she felt threatened.

There was another other tragic truth about the little baby, I participated in killing. The older I get and the closer to God I become, the more this stayed in the forefront of my mind. Most of my life I have been a firm believer in "you reap what you have sown, more than you sowed, later than you sowed." What you do does come back to you in life sooner or later. I've known a lot of people like to point the finger at God; because it's easier to believe we are somehow a victim or being punished. It took me years to come to terms with the reality that we are not victims of the things we shouldn't be doing.

Even as a young girl, don't get me wrong, because the girls I had later in life I always loved to pieces, but I'd always wanted a boy. Mournfully, I've no doubt in my heart—and God has never led me to feel otherwise— I aborted the only son I was ever destined to have. I spent the next thirty-plus years of my life, mothering my brother some of my favorite uncles and cousins, my boyfriends, and every little boy and young man for miles around. Trying to fill the void and need for a son to mother. I never considered how this behavior was often painful to my girls and sometimes seen as some kind of rejection. The fact that I didn't intend for this to happen is not the point. I'm sure it did. Telling someone how much you care or love them is just words. Showing them is a demonstration of genuine love in action. Action tells an undisputable truth that never has to be questioned, bought or proven. To put it like Nana Hammond used to say, "Talk is cheap and good whiskey costs money!" I can only pray that my actions today show the genuine love that I have for my two girls.

The Time Was Drawing Near, and I Wasn't Ready

The bottom fell out of my life after my sixteenth birthday. I felt like I was plummeting down a black hole with nothing to hang onto. It became more obvious daily that my grandmother was failing badly. Her remaining children and Aunt Charlotte were starting to fight over her care and who would be executor of her will. My older sister had moved home with her new baby because her husband had run off with a younger woman. The fighting between Uncle Henry and my brother Jim had reached a desperate point. Nana's house was starting to get destroyed from all the physical fighting. Cabinet doors were punched off their hinges; the only new refrigerator Nana ever had was dented by my brother's fist. Panes of glass in the laundry room and shed were cracked and broken, usually by chairs, during Uncle Henry and Jim's brawling.

Nana would make it through Christmas and part of the winter. In early February she started to bleed from her rectum, and the doctors couldn't stop it. She was admitted to the hospital. I was left alone with raging drunken tyrants; while my older sister and her baby hid in an upstairs bedroom. The day Nana left the house to go to the hospital with Aunt Charlotte, my grandmother called me into the bedroom we shared. Sitting in the big arm chair she always sat in when she couldn't sleep, she said, "Here,

Baby-doll. I want you take my change purse. There's a twenty-dollar bill in it—it's all I have left to my name. But I want you to take it. Only spend it if you really need something."

The next day, I just knew in my heart she would never return. I became crazy with fear by the third day. Consumed with anxiety that she was going to die, I called our family doctor, bawling my eyes out; I begged him to not let my grandmother die. He said with a very calm Dutch accent, "Your poor grandmother is all worn out. I've done everything I can to help her. She's worked too hard her whole life."

That afternoon a big northeaster blew in out of nowhere, and my anxiety worsened by the minute. I wanted to call my father to ask him to bring me to see Nana in the hospital before it was too late. My brother Jim was feeling extra hateful that afternoon, even towards me, which for the most part was unusual. As Jim got older and angrier, he used to beat the tar out my two older sisters. He never made a practice of trying to handle me over, after he had tried it once, because, I laid the back of his head open with a heavy blown-glass vase shaped like a long-necked goose. He never touched me again.

However, he got so huffy about me calling our father. He pulled the phone out of the wall. For whatever reason, he didn't want me to. When he wasn't looking, I bundled up and walk over town in the blizzard to use the phone at the general store. I didn't want to go to Aunt Charlotte's—she was the last person I needed to see. I told the storekeeper, old Mr. Rand, "I need to use your phone real bad. My grandmother's dying, and I have to get to her!"

I called my father's house. He answered on the second ring. I was crying so hard, my eyes were almost swollen shut. The storm blowing outside the store window by the phone had become a white blur. I desperately blurted, "Dad, you have to come get me. You have to come now. Nana's up to the hospital dying. I just know it! Jim wouldn't let me call you from home. I'll wait outside the general store for you." Then I said something to my father I never thought I'd live to say; "I'll kill you, Dad—I'll kill you with my bare hands if you let me down this time. I'll kill you!"

"I'll get there as soon as I can in this storm" was all he said. I felt merciful enough to have my dad stop by the farm to see if Jim wanted to go, but he wanted no part of seeing Nana. I don't believe he could have handled it. Jim was closer to her than the rest of us. Unfortunately, dear old Uncle Henry wanted to go. So, my father, his third wife, my uncle, and I crowded into one of my dad's work trucks. The whole way to the hospital, I kept crying. In frustration, I would frantically yell at my dad to drive faster. The storm was getting worse and more blinding by the minute.

When we finally arrived at the hospital, I bolted out of the truck and almost ran everyone over in the process. I already knew the number of her room and it was a small hospital at the time. I was at her hospital room door in no time. It was closed all but a crack, and there was a note on it that said, "Please check in at the nurse's station before entering." By the time someone responded to me, my dad was standing beside me. Oddly enough, the head nurse somehow identified him as my father.

She told my father we needed to go to the little room at the end of the hall and someone would be in to see us. Within minutes a doctor came in and announced that my grandmother had passed away about thirty minutes ago. I jumped off my chair and ran down the hall and burst into her room. My father knew me well enough to tell the hospital staff not to even try and stop me.

There she lay, nothing but skin over bones, with her head slightly tipped to one side. She was wearing the turquoise V-neck nightgown that she loved. I leaned over and said, "Nana, you didn't have to die now. I'm here now and will never leave you!" Like a dam had been broken, a flood of tears poured from my eyes onto her boney chest. I laid my head down on her stomach; she was still warm. I looked back at the doctor and nurse standing in the doorway and said, "She's alive. She isn't dead." With sober faces, they said, "No, we're sorry. She's gone."

I looked at my dad, who was starting to come toward me, and I yelled, "Don't you touch me, don't you touch me! It's your fault that we didn't get here soon enough!" It was by God's pure grace that I didn't blurt out in that moment that one of the only times I ever went to a party at his house, when I was thirteen, he'd tried to molest me when I went into the camper to get a soda out of the refrigerator. If it had not for Jim catching him, and breaking his nose right there on the spot he probably would have succeeded.

Slowly, Uncle Henry started to wail and walk toward Nana. Filled with rage beyond words, I screamed, "Shut up, you rotten tyrant! You killed her as much as or more than anyone, don't you dare to come near her!" At this point, there wasn't one person in the room that didn't have their jaw on the f loor. And I intended it that way. Without a word, they all walked out of her room and shut the door.

Memories of the only mother I had ever known—Christmas mornings, warm mince pie and back rubs until I fell asleep filled my mind—then mental anguish, unlike any I could remember, consumed my heart as I lay across her chest like a limp dish rag. The biggest piece of me had died. I cried until I vomited. In one fell swoop, my mother, father, and best friend were gone. Seven months and three days later, my eyes finally stopped filling with tears at the very thought of her, or because of the anger and resentment I felt from losing her.

Uncle Henry was clinging onto her at the funeral, chanting, "Mamma, I'm sorry, mamma, I'm sorry, please come back." At one point, he actually sat her up in the casket. There isn't a soul in this world, that couldn't help but have pity on him when Nana died. I know my siblings and I did. In one instant, all the horrific things, he had said and done seemed to dissipate with no effort at all. It was if my heart filled with an almost maternal instinct for him.

After her funeral, my father came back to the farm. As we congregated in the living room I was in shock I didn't know what was going to happen next or what I was going to do. Although, it felt like I had already lived a couple of lifetimes, I was only a little over sixteen. I looked at my father and said, "Dad, what am I going to do? What is going to happen to me?" With no emotion at all, he said, "You're tough—you'll make it. You'll figure it out."

In a matter of weeks the house was closed up and put on the market. None of us had the money to stay there. We couldn't get along well enough not to kill each other, anyway. Of course, I ended up with Aunt Charlotte. My three siblings and Uncle Henry had to fend for themselves, and they did a horrible job at best. Then as fate would have it, the weekend I was set to move in with Aunt Charlotte, her house caught on fire. The top two stories burned, and there was extensive damage to the first floor and basement. They were now homeless too.

I tried going to live with my boyfriend, but to no avail. I will give him credit; he tried harder than I did, but I couldn't forgive myself or him for our decision about the baby. Today as regretful as I feel, at the time it seemed there was no other option. And honestly, I despised his selfish sister. The few weeks I did try staying there, she made me feel like a prisoner that should stay in his bedroom if she was home or when he was at work. After losing Nana, no one or anything mattered to me. My boyfriend's sister made me feel like I was living with another Uncle Henry. Day by day I was getting filled with more and more contempt for her, and for him letting her be so rotten. There was no way it was going to work.

CHAPTER 6

Like the Flip of a Switch

My dysfunctional life with Nana was all that I had known of home and family. Now it was gone. All I wanted was to get out of Lords Hill. I started hating the town. Memories of my life there were deeply rooted in poisonous people and events. I was bitter. Sadly, what had once existed for industry or civic activity and what little else the town offered like a gas station and two general stores, was disappearing in front of everyone's eyes. What didn't die a death on its own was destroyed by some of the townspeople's arrogant attitude of superiority and unwillingness to change.

Having been thrust into adulthood the previous year, I could no longer handle being controlled and nagged at. I became a walking landmine with some people and with others a victim. Feeling completely different from everyone around me and isolated from the rest of the world I started to realize that any control I thought I had over anyone or anything was just an illusion. I had been lied to and told I was crazy for so long I started to believe it was true.

It would take eleven more years before I ended my residence in Lords Hill. Moving a mere five miles away, felt like a different world to me. Perfection will not be found anywhere this side of Heaven, but in my experience, the craziness that sometimes comes with small-town backwards thinking and living is poison to the soul.

Poor Uncle Henry would flounder all about town. It seemed he could not settle down or reside anywhere; his antics were too far over the edge now with Nana gone. When I met him on the street the summer after Nana died, I was heartsick for him, because I knew he had less hope of surviving this life than I did. He was usually broke because someone had exploited his disability money and he was hungry. We were all used to having more than enough to eat—Nana and Aunt Charlotte had always made sure of that. I would give him what little money I had to buy a hotdog and can of soda at the general store. When we parted, I felt like I was abandoning a helpless child. He finally ended up at a relative's house. A woman lived there who was known as black-hearted and evil by the entire town. One day she managed to convince him to blow his brains out, and he did.

I hated life and myself to the point I was more often than not consumed by the desire to be dead. I had not yet recovered from my own horrible mistakes and Nana's death, never mind Uncle Henry's suicide. I worried constantly about my brother Jim. Nana had spoiled him so much, and I had too. Whenever I could, I'd take care of him by buying him clothes and shoes; I'd give him any extra money I could get my hands on.

In the fall when I went to live with Aunt Charlotte, it felt like going from jail to prison. Over the summer I'd started to date a guy whose family had moved to New Hampshire from Massachusetts and bought one of the stores in town. He was good-looking, a little older than me, and very controlling. He ended up being abusive physically and emotionally, and he was extremely jealous. Aunt Charlotte hated him from the beginning. I'd have to lie or sneak out if I wanted to see him.

Although there were some pretty rough times emotionally and physically the year I lived with Aunt Charlotte; I wouldn't have learned all the personal and housekeeping skills I did had it not been for her. I certainly would have given up on any dream or task I endeavored to accomplish but she ruled me with an iron fist. Because of that I was able to achieve my biggest dream: graduating from cosmetology school.

I was the youngest in my class, only seventeen at the time. With some of my peers I was still an easy target for being bullied. Marching into the cosmetology school one day, Aunt Charlotte performed like Nana would have. Guess what? I was no longer bullied! In fact, I ended up graduating with a 97.5 percent average and made many new friends to boot.

Sadly, living with Aunt Charlotte was more than I could bear. I imagine she must have been going through her own horrors after a major house fire right after losing her mother. Regardless of whether she controlled my grandmother's life or not, she had done a lot for us.

From the Frying Pan into the Fire

The biggest disadvantage to living with Aunt Charlotte was being at the bottom of the generational food chain. Some nights, drunk off her rocker, with no warning she'd wake me in the middle of the night to tell me that my siblings and I had killed her mother; we were too much for her, and Nana should never have taken us in. Before leaving the room she'd call me every filthy name in the book! I used to think to myself as she stormed out, *That is a little like the pot calling the kettle black. Isn't it?*

My graduation from cosmetology school came. I had achieved what I had dreamed about. This was the only thing I had wanted since I was in first grade, when I matted my cousin's long hair while playing beauty parlor by teasing it and using a full can of Aunt Geneva's Aqua Net hairspray. It was the only time I thought my Aunt Geneva was going to kill me dead as mackerel, on the spot!

My graduation party at Aunt Charlotte's had to be postponed because she was going away for the weekend with one of her boyfriends. The gift I was to receive for my accomplishment was that man's old car so I would have transportation to go to work and utilize the vocation I had gone to school for.

When she went away that weekend, all I could think about was planning my escape. My uncle worked second shift. As soon as he was gone, my new boyfriend and I loaded my stuff into his pickup truck so fast you would have thought I had never been there. We went to Massachusetts to live in a house his family still owned. I had saved two hundred and fifty dollars. Once it was all spent on food and the other people living there, I was treated like trash and a common beggar.

I tried to get a job everywhere, to no avail. The ones I could get my boyfriend refused to let me take because of his jealousy. The next thing I knew I was being physically abused and threatened worse than I ever had been in my life. Emotionally I felt like a hopeless pile of waste. I had no car and no money. I become almost constantly obsessed with trying to figure out how I could get the one hundred and fifty miles back home.

Finally, when I had the guts to call home, Aunt Charlotte and my uncle were heartsick with worry and felt betrayed beyond words. Aunt Charlotte was too upset to talk to me on the phone, so my uncle told me that they hoped the love I found there was greater than the love I had with them. He added, "You made your bed, so you'd better be happy to lie in it." I was not welcome to live with them again for any reason. I had no doubt that they meant it. I never did live there again.

I Lied and Planned My Escape

I got word that my older sister, who had moved away to Texas with her husband who had joined the service, was moving back to Lords Hill while he went overseas. I knew all my siblings loved me, but the two that were still living in New England were financially and emotionally struggling themselves. I knew when my oldest sister returned, she would be living in a decent place because she had two small children. She and I were always the closest of us girls, and I knew I could live with her. So planning my escape, I lied for all I was worth. I decided to bring only the most important things back to New Hampshire with me. I said "I'm going to visit with my sister because she needs me for a while and is all alone." I never thought before then that I would ever want to kiss a piece of ground that Lords Hill was settled on. However, what I had known was better than where I was.

As we headed back to New Hampshire that day, I was under intense scrutiny from my boyfriend. Barely speaking a word for fear I would trigger him to turn the car around and take me back to the nightmare I had just left, I silently prayed, "Dear God, dear God, help me get all the way home and away from him." I can still see how skeptical and dark his eyes looked as we unloaded my things. My heart was thumping in my chest from unbelievable fear, and I knew my sister could tell I was in an abusive situation. Her face and her arms around me were the most beautiful things I had seen or felt in a long time.

Two more beatings were all I would have to endure at the hand of that boyfriend; because when my brother Jim caught up with him, he remedied that. Aunt Charlotte welcomed me into her home for visits and holidays. So that I could work and take care of myself, she graciously helped me get back on my feet with money for a car and some new clothes.

Within a year I had an efficiency apartment in Lords Hill and was working three part-time jobs. My older sister was struggling because her husband got into a mess in the service and was sent to prison; so I gave her any extra money after my bills were paid. What little I did keep, I used to drink and smoke. I believed in playing as hard as I worked. Aunt Eddie, Aunt Geneva, and Aunt Charlotte tolerated my lifestyle, because they knew how much I genuinely loved them, and almost every night of the week I ate my supper at one of their houses. The rest of the time I lived on macaroni and cheese and packaged noodles.

Meeting My Waterloo

When my emotional pain got to the point I could no longer escape it with alcohol, I went to see the doctor who had delivered me; he had seen me through some less-than-desirable times in my life. By this time he was quite old, but still in practice. The anxieties which had accumulated over the years were now controlling me. Flashbacks from days gone by haunted me. Almost every night I had blood-curdling nightmares. I knew I needed some kind of medication like those I had intermittently taken while growing up. As a child it had helped make what I was facing in the world a little more tolerable. I was able to survive without cracking up. I prayed it would do the same for me now.

Oddly enough I was not afraid to be alone in my little apartment. However, the reality that I was alone in life did frighten me. Any sense of God being with me had long since left. I don't mean that I no longer believed in His existence; I just no longer believed in Him. Before I knew it, I was twenty-one. I had spent nearly three years living alone in my little apartment.

During those three years, I threw more good money after bad into relationships and drinking.. My life had no direction. I felt as useless as I'd always been told I was. I was working, as I use to say "from ding to dong," yet only managed to make enough money to keep on keeping on. If I didn't go dancing at least four nights a week, it was a bad week. In bars was the only time I felt connected with other people. Most of them were doing what I was and for the same reasons: they were lonely and looking for love and happiness.

Then one fateful night, about a week before Christmas 1987, my reckless choices caught up with me. I had just left my third job at the jewelry store in the mall two towns away in the closest small city. It was the Christmas season, so we didn't close until 11:00 p.m. To celebrate the holiday season, the store manager and the other girls thought it would be a good idea to go have a few drinks at a bar on the other side of town before it closed. We chose my favorite lounge, because it had a big dance floor. I drank four beers and six shots of scotch whiskey in under two hours. I danced and laughed and became staggering drunk. The fact that I was exhausted and hadn't eaten anything I'm sure had a lot to do with the extreme change in my condition before I left the bar.

The next thing I remember it was last call and we were all heading out the door. One person said to me, "You shouldn't be driving." I replied, although I could hardly walk or see, "Oh, I'll be all right. I'll see you tomorrow at work." I vaguely remember noticing the light dusting of snow that had covered the ground while we were inside. There had been freezing rain the day before, so some of the leftover ice patches on the roads and parking lot were invisible under the new snow. I skidded slightly on one as I approached my car.

I was cold, tired, and hungry; and I wanted to get home as fast as I could. I was about halfway home when I came to the sharp corner before what is known as Townhouse Hill. I remember looking at my speedometer; it read eighty miles an hour. The next thing I knew, I hit a patch of ice the length of the corner under the dusting of snow. When I hit that strip of ice, my car went airborne about thirty feet, denting three big pines. By the time my car landed, it had rolled over and over; only God knows how many times. I was ejected from the car through the torn-off hatchback and was lying underneath it. The back of my head landed on the edge of the lake. The two front tires were spinning about twelve inches from my face.

I was in shock and still very drunk. Incredibly I crawled out from under the car and walked up to the main road. Staggering down the road, I headed to a restaurant which still had its lights on. A man—I still don't know to this day who he was—came along in a pickup truck. He told me to get in, and then he took me to the hospital in the next town over. He said, "I'm not getting out of my truck. I'll leave you at the emergency room door. I don't need any trouble and you need some help." I have no doubt he was an angel sent by God.

I had a fractured hip and collarbone; broken glass filled my hair. And most of my body was bruised like someone had beaten me with a baseball bat. I had just treated myself to a long wool coat; it was torn and separated at every seam. It looked like someone had taken a seam ripper and removed every thread. The wool panels were just hanging off me. By sheer luck they never did an alcohol test. I knew better than to call Aunt Charlotte, so I had them call my dad. My dad and his wife drove me back to my apartment in Lords Hill. As usual, I was on my own. Anything of value was stolen from the accident scene: my bonus money, gifts of jewelry, and other Christmas gifts which I had purchased. Even my eyeglasses and wallet were gone.

God must have thought, "If this doesn't straighten her out, nothing will." At the time I was still too arrogant to see how longsuffering God had actually been with me. I blamed everyone else in my life for the pain I was in and the way I was acting. I refused to see anything else.

Ouch, that stings not only for the decisions I made back then, but also for the ones that I'm still capable of making to this day.

CHAPTER 7

My Search for Light Resumed

I started visiting God again at the cemetery and at the Episcopal Church in the next town over. They never locked the doors. I started praying with all my heart for a decent person to love me and a family of my own. I wanted children to love, someone to love me and not hurt me, unless I hurt them.

God answered my prayers, but my life would not be void of pain and loss. The recovery and healing I needed to do in the years to come would be more than I had bargained for. In June of 1988 I married my first husband who was sixteen years my senior. He had a good job working for the department of transportation for the state of New Hampshire. He was mature and seemed stable. I believe that he really loved me. However, self-deception caused me to believe he wanted a family, and that the "few" beers he drank were not going to be a problem.

We rented a second f loor apartment after we were married. Guess where? Lord's Hill. Roughly two months later on a cloudy Sunday afternoon I sat on the couch next to one of our living room windows reading something to my middle sister. Suddenly, out the window I saw what appeared to be the ref lection of bright orange that looked like an intense glow from the sun on the side of the building. My husband was in the kitchen shucking oysters and I had three mince pies baking in the oven. In panic I flew off the couch as if a switch had gone off in my brain. Then it dawned on me, "It's a cloudy and rainy day, that can't be the sun." I ran into the kitchen as if someone had shot me and I said to my husband, "Something is wrong out back!" When I opened the door, f lames were already shooting through the window of the back bedroom which we had planned to use for the baby.

Our apartment was in a large five unit building with an empty old horse barn out back. Someone, either by accident or intentionally - this was never determined - had started a fire in the barn. It was an old dry building with animal residue in the wood causing it to go up like an inferno. The ref lection I had seen was from the raging fire.

What few mementos and memories I had from my grandmother, like Christmas ornaments and such had been stored in that back bedroom. Also in there were many of the gifts from my baby shower. I was eight months pregnant at the time and my sister and husband screamed for me to go down the stairs and get out. The outfit I had on, my eyeglasses and pocketbook were all I had time to take. It took only a few minutes for my husband to get my sister and me out. When he went back up the stairs to see what he could salvage, the heat from the fire was so intense it burned his chest before he could enter the apartment.

The Smith family lived up the street. The father and boys were former firemen in town and came rushing down the street. Had it not been for them, nothing would have been salvaged. I stared in horror as I stood across the street on the Methodist Church lawn as they scurried in and out throwing what they could from the front bedroom windows. They tried to get whatever baby things they could before the fire consumed them. The next morning the remainder of my things, about seventy percent, lay in shards of broken glass, soot and water. What could have been salvaged was also lost. That night as we lay in bed at Aunt Charlottes, half a mile away by the way a crow flies, a bright glow woke me from an exhausted sleep. I sat up and screamed like someone had stuck a knife in me. Looking out the window in the direction of our old apartment house, we could see it was in f lames again. Someone had gone in the night and poured gasoline up the stairs to the second f loor and lit it on fire again.

We moved into a lousy little apartment one town away which had once been a store and gas station; it had cement floors and tiny odd windows. My Aunt Geneva washed, mended, and salvaged all she could of curtains, bedding and clothes. For the next five weeks I would have to eat, sleep, and exist on my left side to keep my blood pressure down so I wouldn't cause any harm to my unborn baby.

The day before my twenty-third birthday in late October, I had my first baby, a little girl. Within two weeks the doctor I had been seeing moved back to Pennsylvania. Dr. Mathes would become our family doctor, advocate, and friend for years to come. He would deliver our second daughter, who was born in June 1991. To my dismay, a few months before her birth, I was hit with the reality I had tried to deny: I was married to a full - blown alcoholic. I had believed things would change. The truth was he was very passive-aggressive and self - centered. Sadly I realized too late that he never wanted a family, only a wife.

My life kept marching on from where I had started. In the years ahead, the growth and losses I would endure were often comparable in their severity to my childhood and teenage years. It was still an upward climb, yet, in many ways, better than it had been. I was no longer a trapped child at the mercy of the adults in my life. Dr. Mathes, who always made quality and not quantity of his work the priority, is rare in his profession. His faith in me would empower me to find hope and healing. He did this without masking the real cause of my physical and emotional symptoms with medication. With his strong recommendation, I agreed to see a good doctor of physiology, Dr. Thomas Lynch.

After two years of weekly recovery work with Dr. Lynch, the hills got smaller as I got wiser and learned a little humility. In time, the bridges I crossed became less frightening. With a lot of faith, and the kind of courage that it takes to do the right thing, I'd make it. Suddenly I was at a cross roads in my life where some of my relationships had to change. I was the one who had to choose to make the change if I wanted a better life.

The majority of my family, extended family, and some friends wanted to continue with codependency, abuse, denial, and addiction issues. Most of them chose to believe they didn't have the power to change their way of thinking or their life. It seemed they had no faith in anything beyond their limited selves, prescription drugs, alcohol, and a victim – martyr mindset that had become normal for generations. Regardless of their shortcomings, I still love them. That doesn't mean I condone or share in their lifestyle choices like I used to in order to feel accepted or fit in. Today I'm grateful to God to be able to finally believe and say to myself; "That other people's journey and life choices belong to them and mine belong to God and me alone." I try to remember this without judgment, knowing that God sent Jesus to the cross for them just like He did for me. Being a living sacrifice, or trying to fix a life that belongs to Him and not to me, is stepping on God's toes, thinking we can do His job.

The first half of my life journey may not have always gone according to what I would have chosen, but I have no doubt it was destined by God. I can only hope that sharing my story with others will do some good where it is most needed. I'm hoping to help stop the loneliness and isolation that often comes with abuse and reckless choices. The cruel judgment and lack of self-forgiveness with which the abused and "big" mistake makers often punish themselves, will only create a life full of heavy burdens that can be hard to bear.

Most of us, especially children, do the only thing we know how to when dealing with the hand we are dealt. As a child, it seemed my prayers were all in vain and life was an empty dream. I learned as many children and teenagers do, when we let the desperate part of us control our lives, that we can end up in grave danger! This is what happened to me when I felt more responsible for other people's happiness and survival than for my own.

The Road Got Dark and Scary

After eight years of marriage and my husband's refusing to go to counseling or stop drinking, I knew I had to do what was best for the girls and I. Physical abuse was never an issue. He knew that me would have had him locked up and had the key thrown away. However, the emotional abuse was awful, especially when he was drunk. The tirades that he would go on in front of the girls, or in the kitchen beneath their bedroom, were starting to resemble my childhood days.

Valentine's Day 1996, after my sleeping on the living room couch for the past year, I snapped. With $45.00 and two little girls, I called the local domestic violence program and reached out for help. Before he left work that day, he was served a restraining order and couldn't come home. By this time I had had three small nervous breakdowns and had been telling him for over a year to his face that "I was going to divorce him and find someone else to love the girls and me nad who would treat us right." He never took me seriously. Instead he would tell me, to put it politely, "To shove my counselor and God where the sun doesn't shine."

He used to say, "You have the problem not me. I'm happy. I'm doing fine. You're the one creating a problem, because you're crazy just like your family." To no avail I would try to point out to him that when one person is unhappy and wants out of a relationship, especially when they're married, both people have a problem. To make matters worse, I had been raised in such a way that I knew how to hold my own in order to survive. And I did. The night before he was served with a restraining order, he was drunk as a skunk. He was screaming in our three - year - old

daughter's face; she had taken too big a piece of the turkey I had cooked for dinner and had been unable to finish it. Within seconds of seeing the sheer fright on her little face, I snapped the foot piece down on the reclining chair I was sitting in and bolted towards him. With rather foul language coming out of my mouth, I informed him; that I didn't care if he came home by car, truck, or in a pine box or ever again for that matter. Unlike these kids I'm not trapped here; I can walk out that door anytime I please. But they depend on us to love them and keep them safe. And if I sit by and allowed him to abuse them, then there isn't a nickels worth of difference between us! If he was going to treat them like that they were no longer our children. They were mine!

Spring rolled into summer and he called me relentlessly, begging me to let him come home. After two AA meetings, he thought that eight years of lies and broken promises would disappear like they had never existed. Life just does not work that way. Sorry, hate, and love are only words until we put them into action! My grandmother used to say, "A man is only as good as his word, if his word is no good than neither is he!" When Nana gave her word, it didn't matter if it was a promise to go somewhere or get something, she kept it. If she said, 'You're going to get a beating with the razor strap," especially if she caught you lying or stealing. She meant it!

Don't get me wrong, as my grandmother used to say, "I was no white hen's dove!" I spent money extremely compulsively and racked up credit card debt that haunted us to the end. I gave as my husband used to say; "What we didn't have to give."

After we separated, he started drinking more and becoming more hostile when he didn't get his way. Visitations with the girls were a nightmare. I would usually have to go pick them up before the visit was over. When he had them, he would tell them I was a tramp, sleeping around with all kinds of men. Then he would tell them to ask me who their real father was? He didn't know. If it had not been for my Uncle Frank, we would have lost our home. My husband refused to help me pay any of the bills. He paid only his court ordered child support.

Whenever I did see him or we talked, he'd spew poisonous verbiage at me, trying to put me on a guilt trip. The worst he said was, "that he hoped he would get cancer and die if I wouldn't take him back." In September that year, two weeks before our divorce would be final, he got his wish. He was loaded with cancer. His family and friends treated me like I was a black widow. My setting healthy boundaries, protecting my children, and refusing to be abused were somehow to blame for his fate, instead of the three packages of cigarettes and twelve packs of beer he had been consuming every day since he was nineteen years old.

As it turned out, I was actually the person who became concerned about the decline in his health. He would see our family doctor only if I went with him, and I did. I still loved him. He was the father of my children, and he wasn't all bad. But, I was no longer in love with him. Some people have a way of killing deep intimate love with betrayal, abuse, and manipulation. He was diagnosed with small cell carcinoma (lung cancer), which had already metastasized to both sides of his brain. The doctors gave him three months at the most to live.

His family offered to care for him at his mother's house which he now owned, or at one of their houses, he adamantly refused all their offers. He wanted to come home to be with me and the girls. There was no way my heart could refuse him. I had started to date my present husband, but we agreed to break off the relationship and take another look at it after his passing. My husband drank and was emotionally abusive until a week before he died in a hospital bed in our living room.

One morning while I stood cooking, he sat in his usual chair behind me at the kitchen table. In a sorrowful voice, he said; "Can you ever forgive me for all I've put you through? You know, we'll both be free when this is over." I got choked up as I felt my throat start to close and I said; "I forgave you a long time ago or you wouldn't be here right now." Then as I burst into tears I said, "Oh, why dear God, did we have to come to this!"

The sad reality about un-forgiveness; "is that it's like drinking poison and expecting the other person to die." Instead, it corrodes us from the inside out. I try to remember, if people want to be hateful and rotten, that's on them. I can't be anyone else's keeper. However, once we are old enough to understand life, we need to be accountable. We owe it to God, ourselves, and those around us, not to pass on pain and suffering. I always said, "If what had been done to me didn't feel good, what would make me think it will feel any better, if I do it to someone else?"

On December 14, 1996, as I sat in a chair beside my husband's hospital bed, glaring at our last Christmas tree together as a family; I decided to play the video of our wedding day one last time. He now had a morphine pump in his stomach. Thankfully, his violent seizures, for the most part, had stopped. He could no longer open his eyes. Only the edema that had filled his brain was occasionally trickling from their corners. When the video was over, I laid my sobbing head down on the hospital bed beside his arm. He lifted his left hand one last time, gently resting it on the side of my face. Three hours later he was gone.

For two years after his death, I was out of control. Arrogantly, I turned to the very thing that had taken my mother, haunted my family, and ruined my marriage: alcohol. Using his life insurance money I tried to buy my family and friends, and fix other people's lives with money, in an attempt to ease the guilt that so many people had made me feel because of his death. They cheerfully accepted and borrowed over $200,000. When the last check was written, and the money was all gone I was alone except for my second husband, whom I was still was dating.

Sheepishly, I went to see Uncle Frank one day at his farm in Maine. When he saw me, his face became stoic and blank. Without any warning, he started talking turkey to me and didn't mince his words. Nana Hammond had been like that and most of the people in my family have this trait as well. Sometimes, it's a blessing, or as the case may be, a curse. All I knew was I would have rather died, than lose Uncle Frank's respect. And I believe he knew that! He proceeded to let me know where the rubber hit the pavement when it came to the choices I was making.

Refusing to look me in the eyes, he just stared down at his newspaper. Instantly my heart was crushed and I said, "No, Uncle Frank, I'm not going to keep doing what I've been doing and I going to stop drinking!" He replied, "You can't prove it by me; that's what all alcoholics say." I never touched another drop!

The Upside of Down

The spring of 1999 on Easter Sunday, as my new husband, two daughters, and I were watching a Christian channel that we had recently found, Dr. Charles Stanley's In Touch program came on. Up to this point my church experiences had been limited and unrewarding at best. I knew there was a God and He had a Son, Jesus. Other than that, I was clueless as to who they really were, or what they should mean to me and my time here on earth. I assumed, the Holy Spirit was some kind of a mystical ghost that came to earth to get you when you died.

79

By the middle of the program, we all sat glued to the TV in awe of what Dr. Stanley was telling us. Before I knew it, with no apparent effort of my own, I was on my knees sobbing and accepting Jesus. I had finally been told in a way that I could understand. Over the next twelve years, Dr. Stanley's program was a ritual in our home every weekend. His direct and humble teachings changed all our lives for the better. I owe God a debt for calling Charles Stanley to teach the gospel and Charles Stanley for answering that call!

Three years after this I would lose my dear brother, Jim, in 2002 to a brain tumor. Within the next ten months, Aunt Charlotte and Uncle Frank's oldest son, who worked with my second husband almost every day, would die also. However, I felt very blessed, because my second husband had brought so much love, humility, grace, and emotional security into the girl's life and mine. Most of my family relationships had disintegrated due to the changes I continued to make to break our family's cycle of abuse and codependency. I didn't say perfection. I lived and acted far from perfectly. I am now and will forever be nothing more, nothing less than a sinner saved by God's grace and mercy.

I continued to stay connected with Dr. Lynch. I kept pecking away at my recovery. With Dr. Mathes' wise and conservative approach to medication, as an old timer friend of mine is so fond of saying, "I was able to hold – steady! Finally, in 2004 after purchasing stacks of self-help and recovery books over the years, some that were secular, some Christian based. I found the book and the author that would forever change my life, "I Can't Get Over It" by; Dr. Aphrodite Matsakis. For the first time in thirty-eight years, I had an identity. I belonged to part of the world around me.

I had started to think I was some crazy person with no hope, driven to be a miserable human – being, that derived some kind of pleasure out of having chaos and pain in my life. I was so grateful when I discovered that I had PTSD (Post - traumatic stress disorder). I was my kind of "normal" for what I had been through. At last I was able make some real life - altering progress. And I did it with Dr. Matsakis' program. I was grateful to be able to do some one - on - one counseling with her over the phone and by mail. Dr. Matsakis' program and counseling empowered me to progress faster in six months than I had in the previous fifteen years of counseling.

I have to say, "had it not been for God's mercy and provision of so many wonderful doctors, mentors, teachers, and advocates over the years, I don't know where I'd be today. Commitment and desire had to be my part. The work was hard and the light was often dim, but without a shadow of a doubt it has been worth it. Many times I tried to fix things my way, without God's help and guidance. When I did, it only prolonged the pain and lengthened the time of my troubles.

Only as my faith has grown into a deeper and more dependent relationship on God and His Son, Jesus has my life had the most balance and peace. I know that there will never be a day in my earthly life, where there will not be something I need to be forgiven for, either in word, thought, or deed. That's the way we humans roll. And God knew this: that's why He sent the only perfect person to the cross, so we could be forgiven, Jesus.

As I continue my journey through life, I'm trying to remember that we can try to save those we love from everything, but, themselves! That's God's job, not ours. And being sacrificial emotionally, financially or physically does not spare them the consequences of their own choices. Like I've always told my girls and those I care about; life is like a bank account, we make deposits and withdrawals. It's a kin to the reaping and sowing principle in the Bible. Eventually, either here or on the other side, we will get back with interest what we deposit. Most people want to escape this truth and lay the blame on a cruel and unkind God.

Ironically, these are the people who will tell you at the same time they don't believe He exists!

I often tell people, "Perhaps I am not the best example of Christianity, but I am a much improved version of what I used to be!" Instead of trying to prove who Jesus is by beating someone over the head with scripture that I've memorized, I try to show people who Jesus is, meeting others where they're at and not trying to force them to be where I think they should be. For years I didn't know the answers, sometimes I didn't have any. Hate the sin, but love the sinner is what God's Word tells us to do. We may think we know, but we can't always know for sure what we would do; until we're in the same trenches where other people have been.

My theory is that everyone's life is their own journey. Their fate is based on their acceptance or rejection of God and His Son. It is not my place to be anyone else's conscience; I have all I can do some days to be my own. Any judgment for their choices does not belong to me, nor do I have to answer for them. We become mere shells of what God has destined us to be when we believe that somehow we can be accountable for other people's choices and happiness.

I'd like to leave you with this thought: life for me, thus far has been a journey of many miles, with all kinds of terrain. I can only hope that when I reach glory, my heavenly Father will say, "Well done good and faithful servant, not because, I was a good or always faithful, but rather because I kept trying to fight a good fight! In the words of my dear Nana Hammond, "I've tried to make a silk purse, out of a sow's ear"! God bless until we meet again.

Maggie Miller still lives in a small New England town, with her husband, Michael. Striving to continue to live with humility and gratitude for all the blessings and healing that God has brought into her life, lest, she forgets the road(s) she has traveled in this life.

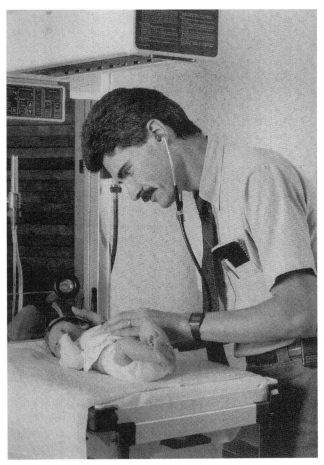

Dr. Mathes with my youngest daughter,
Huggins Hospital handbook June 1991

Colleen Bruce is a woman of amazing strength, courage and generosity. Through over 25 years I have witnessed pregnancies and the birth of her two children, abuse by her husband followed by a cancer death, memories of her childhood abuse and neglect, then the death of her brother and many other traumas. When most people would be overwhelmed or become bitter with repeated assaults on their mind, body and emotions, she has responded with love, caring, resilience and amazing generosity to others. Her struggle and survival should be an inspiration to all.

Sincerely,
Robert J. Mathes, M.D.

Made in the USA
Middletown, DE
20 June 2021